Off-Grid Boaters

One couple's alternative nomad life on a 25-foot yoghurt pot

GLENN BAUER

First published 2020 by Bauer Photography and Media

ISBN:978-1-9163312-1-1

DEDICATION

To my wife, my son, my daughter-in-law, and my grandson.
Oh, and never forget the two fur babies.

CONTENTS

ABOUT THE AUTHOR

As a child, my playground was the wide-open veldt stretched out beneath the blue African sky. Jungle gyms grew naturally from seed, and the pet store was just beyond the garden gate. I wore shoes under protest and then only to school and church. I absolutely needed a bath every night.

After completing high school, I was conscripted into the country's defence force and served as an operational medical orderly or Ops Medic for two years, learning to treat everything from massive trauma to deadly disease. Posted to the volatile border between Namibia and Angola, I was seconded to an armoured policing unit that tracked and hunted insurgents from across the border. When our trackers discovered prints in the sandy soil, the unit would surge into action. Pairs of riflemen would leap from the armoured carriers, racing forward to find the next set of tracks while the vehicles leapfrogged ahead by half a kilometre, dropping off more men to search the ground. All the while, I would be hanging from the side of a jolting carrier, slapping painkillers into the trackers' hands, and urging them to drink. These men would run through the day, eyes wide with adrenalin, ever conscious the next step could trigger a deadly POMZ anti-personnel mine. From behind 50mm cannons, NCO's would watch for the enemy.

A glint of sweat on skin or the burst of an incoming RPG would see the bushveld erupt into a melee of screaming men and flying shell casings while the forest foliage was shredded by cannon and rifle fire.

When it was quiet, I would swim the crocodile-infested Okavango River under the watchful eyes of the men I treated. On patrol, we encountered entire villages which had succumbed to malaria and I would hand out boxes of tablets to suffering mothers. In others, we would be welcomed by the village headman to share the tasty oshikundu beer fermented from pearl millet they cultivated in the fields surrounding their villages.

With my fellow riflemen, we tracked poachers in the acacia forests by day, and at night I listened from my sleeping bag to hunting lions prowling beyond the firelight.

I came away from border duty with a deep respect for the African communities there and could only admire the resilience of people who continued their pastoral way of life as their ancestors had done for generations.

Returning to civilian life, I held an administrative role in a national airline where I met and married my wife. When the opportunity arose, I left to start my own business, which included a second-hand bookshop as well as a postal service which morphed into a same-day freight outfit. With business becoming more fraught each month and with little prospect of it improving, We decided to make a life-altering change and emigrate to the UK. Settling in the South West of England, we raised our son and saw him begin his career in the Royal Air Force.

I have always enjoyed reading, especially historical fiction set in the ancient past. Writers such as Bernard Cornwell, James A. Michener, and Bryce Courtney have played a role in awakening my interest in other cultures and societies. Ever since I was a young boy, I have loved stories and more than that; I have felt a compulsion to write my own. I had tried on and off for years to write, and only really found my groove when I was exploring the Punic Wars fought between Carthage and Rome. Eight years after arriving in the UK, I knuckled down and began writing the Sons of Iberia series. It begins with Warhorn, which quickly soared into the top ten on Amazon in the historical fiction genre. Since 2013, I have self-published seven titles including those in the Sons of Iberia series, available to order from high street and independent bookstores as well as online.

Professionally, I am an Author Member of the Alliance for Independent Authors (ALLi) and a member of the Association of Independent Authors.

As a historical fiction writer first and foremost, my website is primarily about historical happenings centred around the Punic Wars, specifically the Second Punic War.

I support children's education and have an open offer to sponsor tuition to a pupil from a disadvantaged background at Kanaän Centre in Limpopo, South Africa.

Thank you for choosing to read Off-Grid Boaters. I hope you find reading about our somewhat chaotic bid for an alternative way of life enjoyable.

May the tale never grow old,

Glenn Bauer

FORWARD

Jenny Ives is a Chartered Financial Planner specialising in retirement planning. She and her husband are also professional house and pet sitters, and when not looking after homes and pets, either in the UK or abroad, they are out exploring the countryside from the van they converted into a campervan. With their years of campervan experience in different countries and extreme weather, I could think of no one more qualified to introduce a book about living off-grid in England.

It is no surprise to me that Glenn lives permanently on a boat and is happier for it. I have fond memories of a boat adventure of my own with Glenn. As my older brother by four years, he led the charge on our holiday adventures when we were let out of boarding school. One hot African summer we built ourselves a boat. We had found a gigantic piece of polystyrene left behind by the builders of a new reservoir. This formed the base of our vessel and to which we attached rudimentary wooden sides and even a slanted piece upfront as the prow. Armed with one garden shovel as an oar, Glenn scoped out the opposite bank and chose a spot to launch our maiden voyage. We were going to attempt to cross a rather large and deep dam on our homemade craft. Our first threat came not from the water, but from the sky. A hazy cloud materialised into a swarm of African honeybees (the origins of killer bees) many of which tried to land on our raft mid-crossing. Glenn fought them off gallantly, instructing me to splash them. I did this as furiously as I could whilst trying not to capsize us. Apart from a few stragglers, we won the killer bee battle.

The next ordeal felt like a psychological thriller. We spotted a large black snake in the water and to our horror, we were on a collision course with it. Just feet from us, it ducked deep beneath the surface and disappeared under the raft. Captain Glenn appointed me as look-out, and I had to ensure the snake did not try to board the boat. Reaching the far bank, we stood for a moment savouring the accomplishment before thirst and hunger intruded, and forced us to set sail for our home shore. What we thought would be a quick crossing had turned into hours, but despite our safe return, the perils of our adventure were not over yet.

Unbeknown to us our 'trespassing' had been noted by a farmer who got onto his CB radio to advise all and sundry that there was a suspicious-looking craft on the Impofu Dam. The superintendent of the installation, our father, set off with his assistant to investigate. As we beached, a municipal vehicle, rocking and swaying over the rough ground, approached us. We thought we had lucked out and could hitch a ride home as we were sunburnt and shattered. Imagine my father's fury upon discovering that the offenders were his own children. To make it worse, he was compelled to file an incident report about the unlicensed 'boat' commanded by minors without life jackets!

I was still in boarding school when Glenn was conscripted to the South African Defence Force. It was during those years that I came to appreciate Glenn's marvellous ability to craft stories. His letters would arrive in envelopes bursting at the seams. The girls in the dormitory would gather around excitedly as I proudly read aloud the tales of an army medic patrolling our country's borders.

The next border that Glenn would scout and write to me about were the borders of Britain. He and his wife had emigrated with their son and they assured me that England was not always cold, damp and grey. With their glowing accounts of plenty of employment and security, my family followed their footsteps as we migrated to the Northern Hemisphere.

Glenn showed us the ropes in our new home country and smoothed the path for what was a very different way of life. Glenn has a knack for scoping out a situation and quickly finding ways to adapt, and we leaned on his insights as we settled into our new country of residence with ease. I not only changed countries but also my career, having fallen into financial services on arriving in England. Now, many years later, as I sit in the homes of millionaires advising them on their family fortunes as a Chartered Financial Planner and Fellow of the Personal Finance Society, our upbringing in Africa feels like a past life, perhaps even surreal. I know that they happened for those experiences have left their mark on my soul and I see they left their mark on Glenn too. We crave adventure and nonconformity. It was these stirrings that led me to switch up our mundane suburban life for one of adventure through pet sitting and van living, which we have been doing permanently for five years, building up a base of satisfied pet owners. Many people may be surprised to discover that the House and Pet Sitting sector in the UK has become a professional sector. In 2019, I attended the House & Pet Sitting Conference as a speaker in both of my fields of expertise; house sitting and financial planning.

Throughout Off-grid Boaters, Glenn takes the reader down the canals, transporting us along with the adventures and challenges of full-time boat life. They have painted a marvellous story of boating on the waterways of England and have not glossed over the tribulations of boat life. It is in Glenn's nature to furnish others with ways to mitigate challenges through his own experiences. This book provides a blueprint of what first-timers might expect and where potential learning curves could be uncomfortably steep. On reading the book, I am now inspired to swap out a season of van life for one on the canals. What I enjoyed most about this book is Glenn's humour which had me laugh out aloud and makes Off-grid Boaters an entertaining read for new and old deckhands alike.

Fair winds to all!
Jenny Ives
Chartered Financial Planner & Fellow of Personal Finance Society.

CHAPTER 1
PLANNING OUR ESCAPE

The rent trap. Exploring boat life. Taking the plunge.

In 2008, the UK, like the rest of the world, entered a devastating economic downturn. Four long years later, recovery was still marginal, and salaries were frozen. For us, not being burdened by a mortgage was a blessing as, across the country, homeowners saw the value of their property fall. In that year alone, repossessions of property rose by fifty percent to forty-thousand and most of these were owner-occupied. Instead of a mortgage, we rented. Month after month we coughed up a third of our net income to cover the rent, council tax, and utility bills. Family holidays were rare and then always on a shoe-string budget. Our savings grew at a glacier's pace.

Like so many other people, we began to search for a way out of what seemed an endless grind of working to earn only enough to afford the next month's rent and groceries. Over the space of three years between 2015 and 2018, we made increasingly drastic reductions to our expenses in an effort to increase our savings. When my car failed its MOT, I scrapped it and we made do with a single car. When our son left home to begin his career, we moved to a smaller house with a lower rent. When the TV broke, we said good riddance, as much to spare our sanity as to save money on buying a new set and paying the annual licence fee. Going on five years later, and much to my amusement, I still get threatening letters from TV Licensing. The microwave followed the TV set to appliance heaven. Yet, no matter how much we reduced our expenses, it seemed we could never save enough to amass a deposit for a home or to secure an income to support us when we retired.

Inevitably, we had to face the bitter truth. We rented a tiny two-bedroom house that did not belong to us but swallowed a massive amount of our disposable income. If we could only find less costly accommodation, we would be able to save enough to put down a large deposit on a home of our own and enjoy a decent pension. That too was a non-starter. Unless we took a seedy flat in the grimmest parts of town, we could not find a place that cost less than what we were already paying.

Sadly, we were not the only people struggling in this way and many were even worse off than us. More and more people are turning to unconventional places to live. There are people living rent free in empty office buildings in exchange for providing a deterrent to vandals and squatters. Others have turned to tiny homes, and many live in their cars and vans.

Caravans and campervans were an option, and we watched vlog after vlog of DIY enthusiasts turning rusting hulks into pretty nifty living spaces. At one point, I even flippantly suggested we could try living in my car, a roomy Ford Mondeo.

Occasionally we would drive out into the Wiltshire countryside to explore rural villages and sun-dappled country lanes. We often passed over the Kennet and Avon Canal, throwing a casual and somewhat cynical look at the colourful narrow boats moored along the banks. We went for a jolly on one in Bradford-on-Avon, snapping photos of regal swans and the handsome brickwork of the arched bridges. One our work colleagues had a narrowboat moored on the upper Thames and invited us for a day's cruise. We arrived to find her packing away paints and brushes, flushed with the glow of having completed some fulfilling purpose. Seeing us, she proudly displayed a stained-glass window that she had been painting. Lovely. It fitted into what is called a 'cratch board', a triangular frame that supports a canvas cover at the front of the vessel. After a cup of strong tea, we cast off from the grassy bank of the Thames, and with an old Lister engine chugging away in the compartment beneath our feet; we headed downstream. It was a glorious sunny day and every bit as relaxing as it looks. Determined to show us that it was not all butterflies and daisies, our host decided to dock at the local elsan point so we could participate in pumping out the sewerage and refilling the water tank. I scrambled to the bow of the narrowboat and stood ready with a mooring rope as she steered her vessel up alongside the lock landing. Eager to prove my worth, I hopped onto the jetty and looped the rope around the iron bollard while the boat glided on, rope rapidly tightening. That was when I realised that I had used the port side rope to secure the boat instead of the starboard side rope. Too late. Tautening against the full weight of the iron narrowboat, the mooring rope splintered the wooden cratch board and shattered the still-drying stained-glass window. The boat slowed to a stop, a miserly yard too late, and our host jumped onto the elsan landing from the back end of the boat, oblivious to the carnage I had wrought. Mortified, I had to explain to the captain my blunder. She shrugged it off, but it was plain to see she was upset. Feeling awful, I promised to cut a new board for her and took the splintered wreckage home that afternoon to use as a template.

That mishap aside, it was a very enjoyable day on the river. Her boat, while over ten years old, looked comfy inside with all the basics; hot water shower, flushing toilet, gas stove, and wood burner. Still, we agreed that living permanently on a narrow boat was crazy. Winters were long and cold, even with the national grid to keep us warm and dry. How much colder must it be on a boat? We were from Africa after all. Out of the question, I declared. My wife would agree and so this completely crazy idea would be dropped. Then a couple of months later it would resurface.

Another dream we have is to live for a while in France. One evening my wife began talking about the waterways in France and showed me a video filmed along the Canal du Midi. This picturesque canal runs from Toulouse to Étang de Thau on the Mediterranean. As I watched, I became fascinated by the fact that boaters could cruise from far inland all the way down to the coast. Interest now well piqued, I did a quick search online and learned that boats could cruise along the Kennet and Avon from Bristol all the way to the Thames and then on down to the English Channel, cross it to Europe and keep going on canals all the way to the Mediterranean. What sorcery was this? How had I not known this before? This was freedom! The idea that we could visit so many places while travelling in our home was intoxicating. This was a positive counterbalance to the cold, wet months of winter.

It was early 2017, and we had agreed at last that perhaps life on a boat in England was a feasible solution. It offered a way to not only to reduce the ever-soaring cost of living, but to also leave the hustle of living in a large, congested town.

Our savings were modest and we were adamant we would not buy on credit. This meant we'd need to do a lot of homework on boat prices, overheads, fees and other expenses. We started with the basics; the prices of boats, boat license fees, insurance costs, canal rescue insurance, boat fuel, gas, and the additional costs of commuting from out of town to work. Adding these up against the cost of rent and utilities was an eye-opener and even if we underbudgeted, we would still be able to save triple what we could while renting. I have detailed these costs on my website for anyone interested (see the appendix for the web address). We began by almost religiously scanning the popular boat sales websites (See appendix for a list of the ones we found most useful). I even went so far as to set up Google Alerts for the types of boats we thought would suit our needs.

I booked tickets to visit the annual Crick Boat Show, billed as Britain's biggest inland waterway festival, and we duly set off one sunny May morning. Up the old Roman road, the A429, we drummed, bushy tailed and bright eyed. It was not too long before I noticed a sign advising how many traffic accidents had occurred along this stretch of road. A sobering reminder of our mortality and quickly forgotten. Except it wasn't because a few miles later, we passed another warning sign. And another, and another. I was strangling the steering wheel with white-knuckles by the time we arrived at the tail-end of the queue to enter the boat show.

The festival is a much-anticipated event in the UK boating calendar, attracting tens of thousands of visitors from far and wide to the exhibitions, seminars, and of course, the boats. After arming ourselves with a cup of coffee each, we hurried to the first boat ownership seminar. Five minutes into it with my wife furiously scribbling notes beside me, I began to experience a sinking feeling. There was so much to learn! Blacking the hull, measuring the thickness of the metal, and diesel bug. No, that is not a typo. There really are microbes that consider a diesel fuel tank the perfect place to set up home. Oh yes, and their excrement is not at all good for the fuel. People laughed, but I caught the eye of several pale-faced wannabe boat-owners, who like me, were reeling at all the unfamiliar nautical terms.

The seminar concluded and we made a dash for the coffee stall where we drained a couple of americanos. Balance restored, we grinned at one another dazedly and set off to quietly wander through the exhibition stands. This was more my thing. Solar panels, rope fenders, and fancy loos. There were devices of all kinds to marvel over. With a backward glance at all these shiny toys, I was dragged off to the rows of even bigger toys; the boats themselves.

There is something carnival-like about a marina filled with brightly decorated narrowboats and it was not long before we were both caught up in the atmosphere. After an hour of appreciating the many boats on show, I nudged my wife and pointed at a number displayed on the roof of a nearby boat. It had a lot of zeroes. A lot. "We could get a smallholding in France for that price." She pointed at the price of the next boat on. "Or a whole *département* for that."

We joined a short queue to climb the stairs to a brand-new barge that had been craned onto dry land. I ducked through the hatchway and into the boat to find myself staring into a vast open space. Other than the laminated wooden flooring, no fittings had been installed. It was a sail-away, so called because a person could buy it and cruise away to design and fit it out themselves. This was not on my shopping list.

We came away from the boat show with a new sense of what we could not afford. So, pretty much anything built of iron after the turn of the century was out of the question. That said, I had noticed one boat that did suit our meagre budget. It was on a trailer and off by itself in a corner, rather like a poor cousin at a family gathering. I studied the photos I had taken of it with my phone and began to do some research. Unlike the colourful narrowboats, this vessel was built of glass-reinforced plastic (GRP) and was a cabin cruiser. This was a style of boat I was familiar with from occasional fishing trips on coastal rivers in South Africa.

Undeterred, we agreed that spending a few days and nights on a narrowboat would be a good idea. Not only could we have a nice little break, but we could see first-hand if we could cope or even liked it. We found a hire boat company based in Devizes on the Kennet and Avon Canal and secured us a booking for two nights onboard one of their hire boats. September came around and watching the weather nervously, we arrived at the Devizes wharf where we were met by an employee of the hire boat outfit. Wide eyed, we listened intently to all his instructions on starting up the engine, tightening the grease thingy and running the bilge pump.

With the basics covered and the engine growling reassuringly below us, he cast off and took us for a short cruise up the canal. Turning the boat at a winding hole, he passed me the tiller. Steering with a tiller is a bit of a knack as you push or pull it in the opposite direction you want the front of the boat to go. Fortunately, I was not too awful and managed to keep us heading in a straight stripe down the canal. I think he must have decided I had passed the test because he jumped ship at the wharf and waved us off. Heart hammering, I set my eyes on the not-so-distant horizon and assumed a captain's stance as I throttled the engine to a smidge over tick-over speed. Tick over speed is the absolute slowest a boat will go while the maximum permissible speed is a dizzying 4mph. The idea is you chug along at 4mph until you see moored boats at which point you throttle back to tick-over speed so as not to rock the moored vessels. If you neglect to do this, especially if in a hired boat, be prepared to receive some verbal abuse from annoyed boaters.

Cruising at tick-over speed, we grinned happily at one another between staring at the homes and boats that lined this stretch of the canal. A sharp bend slowly materialised ahead and assuming my concerned expression, I ordered my first mate to the front of the boat to act as lookout. Meanwhile, I was eyeing a red button on the dash and my trigger finger was itching. With a cheeky aye-aye, my wife double timed to the front of the boat and peered ahead, ready to repel Vikings, locals, or both. Judging the time just right, I jabbed the red button. Twice. At the front of the boat, my first mate fairly lifted off the deck as the air horn blared its warning to any boats out of sight around the bend. Unfairly, in my opinion, I was told off and advised no tea would be provided until some undetermined time in the far future.

The next two days were an absolute pleasure. The weather was pleasant and the boaters we encountered were friendly. On the second day, I had the hair-raising experience of negotiating between the bank and an oncoming seventy-foot monster all while lining up my approach to a bridge. Somehow, I managed to avoid bumping into any of the obstacles and, knees shaking, breathed an enormous sigh of relief as we passed under Horton bridge. The Kennet and Avon Canal is rough and ready as canals go in the UK. By this I mean it has long stretches of shallow sides that prevent you from mooring snugly against the towpath. I loved it and after a long day of manoeuvring round tight bends and between tall banks of rushes, I fell onto the queen-sized bed, ready to sleep like a log. Just as I was drifting off, a motor kicked into life right under the mattress and cursing like a sailor, I jumped to my feet in fright. It ran for a minute before shutting down. Blinking owlishly in the dark, I realised it was an automatic water pump and no threat. Yes, it switched on and off all night, but after the first dozen times, we no longer heard it and fell asleep.

Mooring along the bank proved to be hit and miss as it was impossible to judge the water's depth. At times we'd moor right up beside the towpath with no problems. On other occasions the hull would crunch along the bottom while we were still six feet from the bank. Bringing the boat to a stop so that one of us could jump onto the towpath and secure us was also problematic, and hammer and mooring pins were brandished aggressively more than once. We cruised up to a tiny place called Honey Street where we filled up the water tank and turned the boat at a nearby winding hole. After two-and-a-half days of decent weather, the skies opened just as we approached Devizes, our final destination. With no windshield or canopy, I got a taste of boating in wind and rain to balance out all the good weather.

With this experience under our belts, we were confident

that life on a boat could be the ideal alternative to renting a house. The canal was close enough to town for us to commute to work. There were plenty of spots we could both moor a boat and park our car. The tranquillity of the countryside through which the canal stretched was just the tonic we needed, and finally, we felt we could manage a boat of our own.

With newfound confidence, we redoubled our efforts to find a boat we could afford, had a reliable engine, and was suitable for living onboard.

CHAPTER 2
SHOPPING FOR A BOAT

Chasing the dream. Test driving a boat. The Thames in flood. Blue skies and calm waters.

Early in 2018, we saw an advert for a cabin cruiser near the City of Bath. It looked tidy and the price was in our budget, if at the top end of it. By this point we were almost exclusively looking at GRP boats. The biggest obstacle was finding a boat in our neighbourhood i.e. on the upper Thames, lower Severn or Kennet and Avon Canal. Most of the more realistically priced GRPs were located up around Liverpool or over in Norfolk. Seeing great looking boats way up north was frustrating. We simply could not afford a three-hour round trip every weekend to view prospective boats.

I was unable to take time off work, and we were loath to miss this opportunity to view a local vessel. Fortunately, my son was able to accompany my wife out to meet the agent and view the boat. It was a 22ft cabin cruiser and the owners had unknowingly inherited it a year earlier along with the estate. It was on the market since they were not interested in boating. They took all of two minutes to realise that the boat was way too small, being both too narrow and too short.

It was an important lesson for us. We would need to see more boats in person rather than relying on the online specs. The solution was to visit the local marinas and wharfs to get an eye for the different sizes and configurations. It was a wet winter and the Thames was running high. At St. John's lock on the Thames, a kindly boat owner allowed us to climb aboard his Shetland. Again, it was tiny and ideal for a bank holiday weekend. Not so much for a liveaboard.

In Pewsey, we encountered a woman with an old 30ft canalboat who was happy to tell us more about what to expect when living on the canal. By this stage we could name half a dozen different boat types and were familiar with the typical configuration of the cabin, galley and deck.

Our ideal boat was a 32-foot cabin cruiser with a centre-cockpit and an aft cabin. I was keen on an inboard engine as opposed to an outboard motor as the inboard could double as a power source for appliances and lights. Also on the list was a gas oven, a shower, a bulkhead between the galley and the fore cabin, and a good canopy over the deck. A recent Boat Safety Scheme certificate (BSS) was an essential requirement. The BSS is like a MOT for the fuel and energy parts of boats. The most likely makes were a Viking or Norman.

I was at the back of the house one night in April when my wife called excitedly that a GRP cruiser had just been listed online. It was down the road from us on the Thames near Lechlade. She was not exaggerating either. It had literally just been listed while she was browsing through the site. The boat was a Seamaster, not one of the makes we were familiar with, but it had the essentials and it needed next to nothing done to make it fit for living aboard.

Our project had just become very real. Here in front of us was a way to break free of the trap of paying rent and being stuck in a gloomy town. My hands became clammy as I looked over the advertised specifications; looking for that one flaw that would make my decision for me. There were none. The boat was good. The air draught would see it fit beneath the lowest bridge on the Kennet and Avon Canal. It was wider than the Vikings or Normans we had been hoping for, but not too wide for the locks or swing bridges. It had a diesel inboard engine, a current BSS, shower, gas oven, separate sleeping cabin, a hardtop above the cockpit, and a reasonably good canopy. It was incredible, and it needed to be seen. I nodded, heart in throat, and we shakily sent an enquiry to the seller. He responded fifteen minutes later and we set up a time to view the boat the following evening after work.

It had been a wet winter and the rain had only just begun to clear up. Fortunately, there was plenty of light to negotiate a muddy track through a farmer's field to the private marina on the upper Thames where the boat was moored.

Reciting all the parts and aspects of the vessel we needed to remember to check, we met the seller who was waiting for us on the jetty beside a bobbing Seamaster 25. The first thing that struck me was how much bigger she seemed compared to many of the GRPs we had seen moored along the canal and river. The second was that she needed a good scrubbing. It was evident that beneath all the flaking paint, moss, and lichen was a proud vessel. While we looked about, the buyer primed the engine with fuel and started it up so I could appreciate the throaty rumble of the 29HP *Nanni* diesel. Again, it was not an engine I was familiar with, but it was just a few years old and looked formidable.

Also impressive was the galley, saloon, fore cabin, and head. The gas cooker, oven and grill were in good shape and the shower had hot water, curtesy of a calorifier connected to the engine.

The vessel's name was Wyebourne, and it seemed to be ideal. Trying to appear cool, we agreed to a 'test-drive' that Saturday if the water levels on the Thames would allow it. One thing that had been reinforced at the seminar we had attended the previous year was the importance of hiring a professional surveyor to check any boat we planned to make an offer on. So, the following day, I called up a boat surveyor who gave me a price to do the survey and the number for a boatyard who could crane the vessel out of the water. By happy coincidence, the owners of the boatyard were familiar with Wyebourne and gushed about her. They advised that the engine especially was sound and that the boat had been overwintered out of the water at their yard two years earlier. Reassured by their glowing detail of the engine and hull, I decided to ignore established wisdom and forego the boat survey.

Excited by the knowledge that the boat was in good condition, Saturday came around all too slowly. By then, the river had subsided somewhat. The seller already had the canopy down and engine running when we arrived. Greeting us on the jetty, he gave us permission to board the boat and I thought I detected a hint of nerves. I watched everything he did like a hawk, not because I suspected anything devious, but because I wanted to learn as much as I could. He brewed us all a cup of tea while we stuck our noses in every cupboard, under the cots and beneath the carpets.

With a steaming cuppa each, the seller then gave us a short safety spiel, showed us how and where to cut power to the engine in case of an emergency, and where the lifebuoy and fire extinguishers were stowed. He was a leisure boater. In the five years he had owned Wyebourne, he had used the boat just once or twice each summer. I realised that his nerves were due to a combination of being a little rusty with handling the boat, our presence, and the exceptional river current. Better cautious than foolhardy, though.

It was sunny, if a little cold, as the seller cast off and carefully steered Wyebourne out from between her neighbours. I noticed that they all wore a winter-weary patina, which made me feel a little better about the patches of green moss and grey lichen on Wyebourne. The boat was equipped with a suitably handsome wheel which made up for the mouldy captain's chair. Our captain turned to the starboard and into the current. To my inexperienced eye, Wyebourne seemed to handle well and so when I was offered the wheel, I stepped forward with just a flutter of nerves. In the UK, there is no requirement for the equivalent of a driver's licence to pilot a boat on inland waterways and I was keen to see how a cabin cruiser handled in comparison to the narrowboat we had hired the year before. My first impression, standing there with the wheel in my hands, was that the boat was huge. It was nothing like driving a car where you can see the road surface a few meters beyond the bonnet. All I could see was the cabin roof stretching out before me while the river lay well beyond the bow rail. After I had adjusted to the scale of the vessel and the river, I began to enjoy the experience.

We cruised upriver to St. John's Lock, where our captain took the helm and guided us into the slimy confines of the structure. A lock keeper was in attendance and he did all the work of tying us up and operating the lock paddles and gates. Again, I paid careful attention to everything he and Wyebourne's owner did.

On the trip back downriver, I left my wife with the seller on the deck and went inside the boat. I wanted to give the interior a more critical inspection. After all, this would be our home if we followed through. I looked for telltale signs of water ingress, mould, or any other potential issues. The windows were well sealed. The gas cooker included two gas burners, a grill, and an oven. Sniffing, I couldn't smell any gas and the unit looked spotless. Not five minutes later, I felt the boat turn sharply and the engine revs increase. A heartbeat later, there was a crunching and splintering from above. I popped out onto the deck to see that the seller had taken over the steering. There was a carpet of green leaves laying on the deck and twigs everywhere. An overhanging branch had caught on the hardtop of the canopy, but there was no damage. The seller's nerves had faded somewhat by this point, and he was at last enjoying the outing. Consequently, he increased speed and I was suitably impressed at the responsiveness of the steering and the engine. It was no speedboat, to be sure, but neither did the diesel engine feel sluggish and the boat fairly glided along.

Back at the marina, it was decision time. There was another vessel near Oxford on our shopping list and we had a viewing scheduled for the following day. Wyebourne, though, had made her mark on us. She had everything we needed, was within our budget, and did not need a jot of work done to make her habitable. There was no way we were going to lose her and so after a quick negotiation, we settled on a price that made both parties happy.

How do I describe that feeling that envelopes you after you have made a positive and life-changing decision? Walking on clouds is probably the closest to describing my emotions. I know for a fact that my wife was beaming as we shut the car doors and high-fived one another. 2018 had started off wet and sombre. It had grown gloomier when my position in the small firm I worked at was threatened with redundancy. Instead of waiting for the axe to fall, I had opted to take the package offered earlier that month. The timing was perfect and with the purchase of Wyebourne; it felt as if the sun had come out blazing and indeed; it had. April ended with bright blue skies and me without a job. At least we would soon own a boat that we knew next to nothing about.

My first week out of work had gifted me with ample time to sort out the license requirements, insurance, and river recovery service. There was also the matter of moving the boat from the private marina to arrange. The seller mentioned we could perhaps retain the mooring until later that month when we were ready to begin the voyage down the Thames and onto the Kennet and Avon Canal. To be permitted to remain moored at the marina meant we would need to be interviewed by the Commodore in charge of it. I have never been a rule taker and the need to be interviewed had both of us in stitches. Instead, we found a marina downriver that was quite happy to offer us a temporary mooring for a moderate daily fee until we could move into our new home permanently.

We paid for and officially took ownership of Wyebourne on the first Saturday in May. My son arrived to accompany me on the first leg of the journey, a short cruise downriver to the marina at Radcot where my wife would meet us.

Heart in mouth, I started up the engine, dropped the canopy and bounced around in a state of nerves, trying to remember all the checks I needed to do. When I had run out of excuses and could not delay any longer, I gave my son the nod and he cast off. With eyes like saucers, I slowly throttled the engine and edged Wyebourne out of her berth. Acutely aware of the rows of pricey cruisers moored to either side, I steered my new home out of the marina and onto the river without mishap. I could at last unclench enough to give my son a stern look for his amusement at my nerves.

My wife greeted our arrival at Radcot by waving to us from the bridge that crossed the Thames there. Our mooring was a spot along the banks of the Thames, and I knew enough to know that I needed to bring the boat around and moor up facing into the current. Gauging the angle to bring Wyebourne into the bank, when to slow down, and when to reverse thrust was another steep learning curve. Somehow, I managed to get her up against the bank and my son jumped ashore with a mooring line.

We were beaming like maniacs as we examined every inch of the boat, inside and out. It was incredible. This piece of floating fibreglass and marine plywood, 25-foot long and 9-foot wide, was to be our home. Ahead of us we had so much to learn about the boat, the waterways, the people we would meet and the challenges of life as *Continuous Cruisers*. The first lesson was how to cope with separation anxiety. The boat seemed so vulnerable, bobbing there on the current with strangers walking past it. Locking the cabin door, we then zipped up the canopy. Then we double and triple checked the mooring lines and finally, with many a backward glance, made our way to the car.

The following morning was lovely and sunny, and we got down to Wyebourne early. What a relief to see her sitting serenely on the river. We were keen to give her a thorough clean before taking her for a short cruise downriver. The process of priming the engine, ensuring the water inlet for the cooling system was open, and tightening the greasing gland was straightforward enough, although still unfamiliar, and I did it all just as shown. I turned on the master switches and then the ignition key and a high-pitched buzz sounded. This was normal and indicated that the glow plugs were warming up. After a minute, I turned the ignition key all the way and the engine purred into life.

Casting off was not as simple. The boat was tethered at bow and stern to mooring pins we had hammered into the bank. We had no idea which to loosen first. Since my wife was averse to steering, it fell to her to untie us and pull up the pins while I held the boat in place by nursing the throttle. She did so without any problems before nervously springing from the bank onto the side of the boat. I then turned Weybourne across the current and aimed the bow downriver.

Cruising sedately along, we passed all manner of cabin boats and narrow boats moored along the banks. Once we were beyond them, my wife felt confident enough to take the wheel and begin getting the hang of steering. Unlike with a steering tiller, the wheel on a boat is like a car steering wheel. If I want to turn left, I turn the wheel to the left. The trick is not to overcompensate but to hold my course by making gentle corrections. We quickly learned that the slower we cruised, the more the need to correct our course. We had a fun half-hour of tension as, biting her lip, she tried to get to grips with steering Wyebourne. My own inexperience was not helpful, and it was really a case of the blind leading the blind as we zig-zagged downriver and upriver. I did notice a pattern as we went; like a beginner bicycle rider, she tended to aim for large objects on the riverbank. As the tension increased and the zig-zags became more erratic, I was forbidden from saying anything except to which side she needed to turn the wheel. She would ask, "What side?" and I would respond, "Left. Left! Other left."

Spying a large tree upriver, I began anticipating our course. Sure enough, she headed straight for the tree, eyes growing wider and face paler, until she threw up her arms and flung herself onto the rear bench.

In a rather subdued mood, we cruised upriver to our mooring and made tea. At that point, I would have boarded a man of war single-handedly for a pint of rum. Tea having revitalised us and with a renewed sense of our mortality, we spent a few more hours dusting and clearing out.

Between us, we dragged out a library's worth of romance novels from beneath the front cabin's cots. Rooting around under the storage compartments, I discovered what I thought were bottles of flammable resins. The seller had included a couple of storage bins full of marine DIY products, and I thought the resin was probably some kind of coating for the hull. I fished out two of them and set them with the junk we intended throwing away. Fortunately, when I began tossing it all into the boot of our car, I took another look at the two bottles. Apart from the orange fire hazard stickers, the labels were illegible. The contents had set, reminding me of Plaster of Paris. It was then that I realised what the bottles were. They were ballast and were needed to trim the boat's weight so that it floated evenly and cruised in a straight line (under experienced hands). Sheepishly, I replaced them under the bins to do their work.

Tired and hungry, we headed back to Swindon. Passing a popular fast food takeaway, we agreed we did not have the energy to cook and turned into their drive-through lane. My wife communicated our order through the intercom while I browsed the files of boat literature the seller had given me. As I did so, the crackly voice of the waiter came through the intercom with what on any other day would be a reasonable question, "What side?"

I looked up in time to see my wife's face grow red as she was transported back to the deck of Wyebourne with a monster tree looming. "What do you mean, what side?" She snapped.

"He means mash, gravy or salad." I hurriedly explained, picturing the face of an utterly bewildered teenage employee.

CHAPTER 3
DOWNSIZING TO A SUITCASE

Frayed nerves. Clearing twenty years of furniture.
Goodbye to rental accommodation.

We had been model tenants for three years with never a late payment and the house kept as clean and tidy as the decaying fittings allowed. I remember vacuuming behind a sideboard one day and seeing what looked like little white grubs. At first, I thought they had fallen from the fresh lilies we often put in a vase there. On closer inspection, the grubs turned out to be threads from the ancient carpet.

When we moved into the house, while clean, it smelled overpoweringly of a favourite food dish. We never said a word to the agency, opting instead to open the windows, sprinkle bicarbonate of soda liberally everywhere, and vacuum. It was a November when we moved in and from the first week of occupancy, the hot water was temperamental. I mean temperamental as in there was rarely hot water. So, while we suffered intermittent hot water and heating in winter, guess what? The rent still had to be paid on time. In full.

The grouting around the bath and between the tiles was crumbling away and in places missing. The heating and hot water had worked at some point because the plasterboard behind the tiles was soggy and the preferred breeding grounds for tiny gnats. Whenever I went into the bathroom, there would be half-a-dozen of them flying in erratic circles above the bath or crawling across the tiles. I put an end to their little colony with a tube of grouting; sealing all the tiles and denying entry to the mouldy wood beneath. Unsurprisingly, the generations of spiders that had lived off the gnats were appalled at the loss of their primary food source and moved off. To our bedroom, mostly.

This is what we were leaving behind. There was no sense of loss or melancholy, of that you can be certain. There was a sense of being done over one final time, though. I called the letting agency to give a month's notice first thing Monday morning. The response was an emphatic refusal to accept the notice period. Instead, we had to give a month's notice from the anniversary of our signing the contract. I dug out the rental agreement and sure enough, the said clause was listed. I called back and asked even more nicely, offering to pay a pro rata rental, but to no avail. The conduct of the home rental industry in the UK is as medieval as the car insurance sector. Inwardly seething when all my polite pleading failed, I gritted my teeth and vowed to never again rent.

On the upside, we had six weeks in which to reduce the accumulated possessions of twenty-five years of marriage and raising a son to just a few boxes. How do you even begin to do that? There was no room on Wyebourne for even the smallest piece of furniture, and we could have built a new boat with all the photo frames alone. Exaggerations aside, there were a lot of hard decisions to make. What to keep, what to store, and what to dispose of. The reality was we could only take our clothing, some bedding, a single box of kitchenware, and a small bag of personal possessions each. It might sound reminiscent of a forced evacuation, but I found it liberating. My wife less so.

Offloading a houseful of furniture and appliances in

today's throwaway society isn't that easy. I really didn't want to do a boot sale and besides, we only had a small hatchback. Cue social media. I began to photograph and list items on the local for sale groups, using my social media marketing experience. It worked and the furniture began to dwindle sooner and faster than I had even hoped.

Sticking to the basic tenants of selling, I took lots of photos of the items from all angles. Once I had determined on a realistic price, I would list the item including any and all flaws. Adding a couple of hashtags to make it more discoverable, I'd post the item in the early evening so people would spot it as they commuted or once they had arrived home. I discovered that there is an almost unnatural need for chest of drawer sets. No sooner was a set posted when my mobile would begin pinging with messages from eager buyers. The house began to empty, revealing more of the ghastly 1970s carpet than we cared to see.

I spent hours in the garden, pruning, mowing and weeding. Gutters polished and windows sparkling, we counted down the days to the big move. The day we would move onto our twenty-five feet of floating freedom.

The red-letter day was less than two weeks away, May 18, 2018. That was the day we would move onto the boat and begin a new chapter in our life. It could not come fast enough and at the same time it felt like we were running out of time to get everything done. We especially wanted all the large pieces of furniture gone. On the last remaining weekend, I had lined up buyers for most of the items. I desperately wanted someone to take our two-seater reclining settee. The thing weighed a ton and I dreaded having to load it into a van to take to the recycling depot. As luck would have it, a young bloke messaged me about it and I agreed he could have it for free provided he collected it. Our neighbours must have been all agog at the number of vans rocking up at the house. Inevitably, there came the moment when three individuals arrived simultaneously in their vans to collect the last chest of drawers. I briefly toyed with holding an impromptu auction, but judging the mood, ditched the idea.

It was a humid Saturday afternoon and I took a quick drive down to the recycling depot with the garden waste. Returning home, I discovered that my wife had sold our Chesterfield settee to a young woman who had come on her own to collect. Already perspiring freely, I was soon gasping like a fish out of water while trying to manoeuvre the blasted thing out the back door. It had never been comfortable and apparently it was determined to retain that reputation to the bitter end. Then, like a game of Tetra, The Impossible Level, both my wife and the young woman watched as I tried to get the settee into the back of her car. Ten minutes later, I conceded defeat to the two foot of settee still sticking out from the boot. It would not fit. On the off chance, I tried it in the back of our little Honda Jazz and hey presto; it slid right in. Swaying in the sun, I offered to take it to the buyer's home and she happily agreed. Too late, I realised that my wife had slid the front seats all the way forward. This explained why the settee had fitted so neatly. So, with knees under armpits, I drove the mile or so over to the buyer's home and unloaded it at her front door.

My wife went to work each morning while I focused on our strategic withdrawal from life in a house and a town. There were a million things that needed to be done on top of all the usual daily chores. If the daylight hours were filled with emptying the house, the nights were spent planning our new life and the mission goal was to cruise down the Thames from Radcot to Reading. At Reading, we would leave the Thames and head up the Kennet river on the Kennet and Avon Canal. To where? We had no one place in mind since we were not buying or renting a residential mooring. One of the questions we are often asked is can we legally live on a boat without a residential mooring? We are so fortunate in the UK to have access to a vast, well-developed waterway system. Living onboard a boat has become more common too, and it's estimated that twenty thousand people live on boats in the UK (source: thisismoney.co.uk). Legally, all we need to do is apply for an annual license to cruise, obtain third party insurance of at least £1,000,000 on the boat, and ensure Wyebourne has a current Boat Safety Scheme certificate. There is the option of renting a residential mooring, but they are so few and far between that it is not realistic. Plus, I had already vowed not to rent again. Instead, like thousands of others, we planned to cruise the waterways in accordance with the Canal and River Trust's *Continuous Cruiser* stipulations.

I can't tell you how many hours we clocked up viewing satellite images of the river and canal courtesy of a dominant internet search engine. I also harboured a mounting fear that the river would be too high for us to pass beneath the rail bridge in Oxford. With big eyes and a wagging finger, the previous owner had warned us that navigating beneath this bridge was touch and go due to the low clearance. His tone and the gravitas of his expression had convinced me to take him seriously. Upon doing some research, I calculated that a fluctuation of just 15 inches in water level would prevent us from passing beneath the bridge. Nightmare visions of jamming under Osney Bridge were generally the last thoughts I had every night before I fell asleep. If you've ever seen a boat being swept under a bridge during a flood, you'll understand my fear. It rarely ever ends well for the boat.

We have a large allotment where we grow our vegetables every year. I used the conservatory at the house to start off the seedlings. By May, I had them all planted out at the allotment and I could clear out the conservatory of all the extra pots and shelves. Now I just had to drop off a couple of loads at a charity shop and then take the junk to the recycling centre. Two trips to the local branch of Barnardo's accounted for all our kitchenware, gadgets, and books. I hired a van for the morning and lobbed our beds and mattresses into it, along with bags of junk. This was the last of it all and I took great pleasure in single-handedly tossing every item into the council skips.

A related question we are asked is about council tax. Since it is a tax on domestic property levied by the local council and boats are classed as possessions rather than property, council tax is not levied on boats. Regardless of whether a person lives on it. Sadly, this seems to agitate a certain type of person who feel that boaters forfeit all rights because they do not pay this tax. I've often wondered if they feel the same about the numerous corporations who avoid their tax responsibilities by registering in offshore tax havens. In any event, boat license fees contribute to the Canal and River Trusts combined council tax and business rates tariff as do our winter mooring fees.

The house was spotless. Inside and out. We even engaged the recommended carpet cleaning company to shampoo and wash the carpets, although I had my doubts there'd be any pile left after they were done. We had been stung once before by a landlord who had kept half our deposit and were determined not to let that happen again. Clipboard in hand, my wife met the agency representative who came to inspect the house at the door. Taking charge, she proceeded to guide the agent through the house, pointing out all the pre-existing faults as per the original signed contract. Our deposit was subsequently released and we were free of our rental agreement. We were boaters. With barely any experience of boating, we had taken the plunge and joined the world of nomads and travellers.

Were we afraid? Yes. I tease my wife by calling her WCS or Worse Case Scenario because at times it feels that she expects the very worst to happen. For my part, I am optimistic, sometimes blindly so. Was what we had committed to unwise? Perhaps. We had no contingency plan and we had sunk a large chunk of savings into purchasing the boat. Since being made redundant at the end of April, I had attended three interviews but not secured a new job and so we only had my wife's income and our precious savings to live off. On the other hand, our outgoings had been reduced by over a thousand pounds a month and I was positive I'd find work again within a few months. What we did have was a sense of adventure and excitement. We were backing ourselves to make a go of this new life. We had done it before when emigrating to the UK years earlier. We were doing it again in becoming liveaboard boaters.

CHAPTER 4
WEIGHING ANCHOR

The river level drops. Cast off. Throw a rope. Our first lock. Osney Bridge. Lots more locks.

Radcot Bridge across the River Thames has stood since the 1200s. Being of strategic importance, numerous battles were fought around the bridge and village during England's turbulent past. Now, as I sat on the deck of Wyebourne, splicing and tying knots in rope for the boat's fenders, I watched as a modern-day battle unfolded on the bridge.

The north approach to the bridge is a sharp left turn and, on this morning, a large fuel truck arrived from that direction, gears grinding and engine growling. The driver slowed to a stop. For a moment, I thought he would reverse and cross elsewhere. Instead, he began a thirty-minute exercise to prove that his tanker was as nimble as a Morris dancer. In the blink of an eye, a crowd of experts arrived. Arms waving, they all began to shout contradictory instructions. It was the equivalent of when a person inserts a key into a door and is not at once able to unlock it. Strangers from as far away as twenty feet drop what they are doing to come running, convinced that they alone will be able to turn the key. It as though there is a prime directive hard-wired into our genes. I can just imagine the length of the queue of hopefuls lined up to draw Excalibur from the rock. And I know there was a queue since this is England and we are proud of our queues.

All the while, cars backed up on both sides of the river. After ten minutes, the crowd dwindled to just a pair of unlikely looking lads. The rest had noticed the nearby beer garden opening and raced to queue there. After a further twenty minutes of incremental gains and losses, the driver conceded defeat and was forced to retreat back to the north. Battle over.

On Friday, 18 May 2018, I packed our little blue Honda with everything we thought we'd need for the five-day trip down the Thames and up the Kennet and Avon Canal. Oh, how naïve we were.

Leaving Swindon, we were more nervous than excited. We each had a million doubts and fears. What if the boat's engine broke down? How would we manage the locks? What if the river flooded? Where would we moor up each evening?

What we did not count on was the nasty thumping that began to sound from the front passenger side wheel. Is that not typical, though? We worry ourselves silly over all sorts of imagined catastrophes, only to be blindsided by something we had given no thought to. I gave my wife a pasty smile as she bit her nails. I guessed it was a wheel bearing and reassured her it would be fine for the forty-minute journey. Still, it was another entry on our ever-growing list of expenses.

We duly arrived in Radcot and unpacked our worldly belongings from the car and onto our new home. It was a beautiful late spring evening and since we were moored opposite Ye Olde Swan, we strolled across the bridge to enjoy a dinner there. As it happened, the place was pretty much booked out for a private bash. The staff were lovely though, and very helpful. Between serving the partygoers, they hustled up burgers and fries for us to enjoy in the beer garden. It was bliss sitting there, overlooking our new home bobbing serenely on the current.

"And at my feet the pale green Thames lies like a rod of rippled jade." Oscar Wilde

I wish I could say I drew the Oscar Wilde quote from memory, but I did not. I found it online and thought it fitted the occasion perfectly.

With the party growing in volume, we sat for a while, enjoying the atmosphere and the night sky. When we did return to the boat, I felt it surreal that our home was on the doorstep of an English country pub and on a river steeped in history. This was a feeling that I'd come to experience often as we cruised down the Thames and onto the Kennet and Avon Canal.

To plan our voyage, we referenced River Thames & the Southern Waterways, Waterways Guide 7, a Collins Nicholson Guide. Another resource we used to help us in planning our stops was an online canal route planner. This was useful in estimating how many days a journey would take, how many locks we'd pass through, and where the elsan points were situated. Back on Wyebourne, we reviewed the journey ahead. The plan was to cruise down the Thames as far as Eynsham Lock and visitor moorings on the first day and moor up there. Between us and our destination were six locks. The thought alone was enough to make my hands clammy.

Dawn found me staring east, in the direction of our day's journey. Moments before the sun rose, a cluster of black dots appeared, silhouetted by pinks and reds. They resolved into approaching geese, their honks lifting the hairs on my arms just as the sun rose. The day was going to be a warm one and the rising sun quickly burned off the river mist and dried the dew.

After a mug of strong coffee, I lowered the canopy and tucked it away behind the stern benches. With a deep breath,

I started up the inboard diesel engine. While the engine warmed up, my wife began to untie the mooring ropes and bring the pins onboard. The river current quickly claimed us, and I allowed it to turn the boat about before gently throttling the engine and beginning the long-anticipated voyage. We slid over the silver-gold water, barely raising a wake as we passed moored cruisers, narrowboats, and barges. The early morning air was invigorating and went a long way to calming our nerves. As did the tranquil countryside.

Radcot lock appeared ahead and I slowed to a crawl as I angled up to the lock landing. My wife sprang off the boat and I threw a mooring line to her. The locks on the Thames are generally manned by lock keepers. However, that morning the lock was deserted and there was no sign of anyone on duty. We stared, bug-eyed, at the intimidating gates and paddles. Sure, operating a lock is not rocket science, but it would have been nice if a lock keeper was there that morning. There was nothing for it but to get on with it ourselves. Ensuring the bottom paddles were closed, we opened the top paddles and at once the river roared into the empty lock, quickly filling it. We slid the gates open and I then brought Wyebourne in, taking her to the bottom gates to avoid the lock cil. With the gates again closed, my wife opened the bottom paddles one at a time to drain the water while I held on to the mooring ropes for grim death as Wyebourne shuddered and shivered. Twenty minutes later, we were through our very first lock, having double-checked the paddles were closed behind us.

At Rushey Lock, the next one down, we were relieved to see the gates open and a silver-haired lock keeper waving us in. It probably took him all of a minute to clock that I was inexperienced at manoeuvring the boat and that together, we were winging it. The gentleman was a fount of wisdom and happy to give us all the advice we needed. Naturally, he made operating the paddles and gates seem dead easy. His parting advice was that we should learn to throw a rope and that he still recalled the great fights he and his wife experienced on their first journey. Thus reassured, we continued downriver.

As we cruised down the Thames, the locks grew progressively larger and switched from manual paddles to electric. Fortunately, lock keepers were present at these and on each occasion, we rattled off questions, sponging up every tip we could. Passing through Eynsham lock, we were pleased to see vacant space on the visitor moorings on the south bank, while on the opposite shore, a group of youths shrieked and splashed happily in the shallows. We had survived our first day of cruising.

We did not need a fancy memory foam mattress to sleep well on Wyebourne. The gentle buoyance of the river was all it took to lull us into a deep sleep. That and the sheer exhaustion that comes with travelling and concentrating. The sun rose through a heavy mist the following day, lending a mysterious quality to the early morning light. Refreshed, I stood on the bow, coffee in hand, to appreciate the sunrise.

After competing with the youth group to get some time in the Environment Agency toilets and showers, we were ready for day two. This was the day I would discover if Wyebourne would fit beneath Osney Bridge. Would my nightmares become a reality? How close should I get to the bridge before committing? I had read countless stories online of boaters struggling to pass beneath it. The one that really caught my fancy was the bloke who set up an inflatable paddle pool on the bow of his boat. He filled it with two-hundred litres of water and the weight helped lower his vessel enough to pass under the bridge. I did not have a paddle pool, but I had filled our two hundred litre onboard water tank.

The first test came on the outskirts of Oxford, where Godstow Bridge crosses the Thames. The bridge crosses at an angle which required some nimble manoeuvring of the vessel to pass between the support arches. This was not difficult with Wyebourne, which is only 25-foot long, but we did not count on how low the bridge was. As we cruised beneath it, it seemed lower and lower, and at the last-minute my wife's nerves failed and with a yelp, she ducked. In the shadows, the close confines heightened the rumble of our engine noise, but we had a good foot of space above the hardtop on the deck.

We cruised on, growing more nervous by the minute as Oxford grew around us. Following the course of the river as it curved to the right, I caught sight of the bridge that had given rise to so many of my nightmares. What were they thinking, building it so low? Seriously? To my added horror, there were pedestrians crossing the bridge and what looked like flats or offices on both banks. I was going to have an audience for when I sheered the top of my boat off or became wedged under the bridge and sank.

My wife bravely raised her mobile phone and prepared to film the onrushing calamity. I whispered a prayer and corrected my course, centring up the bow of the boat with the sunlight beyond the bridge. In preparation for this adventure, I had used a weighted string to measure the maximum height of the boat. Then I fitted a bracket to the bow rail and inserted a thin rod which rose to a half a foot higher than the highest point of the boat. Using this rudimentary gauge and targeting setup, I hoped this would give me time to stop and back up if it scraped the underside of the bridge.

With two sets of jaws gritting teeth, we held our breaths and braced. The bridge loomed and I forgot all about overlooking windows or watching pedestrians. The rod cleared the underside of the bridge by mere inches and then the shadow of the bridge swallowed the forward cabin, followed by the cockpit with us in it. Footage from my wife's mobile abruptly cuts to her feet as I throttled the engine, knowing the propeller would dig the rear of the boat deeper into the river. The engine thundered about us, reverberating deafeningly off the underside of the bridge and supporting columns. Then we were through, bright sunlight falling on us and our hearts lifting.

I am not proud of it, but at that point, I did turn and flip the bridge the bird and bellowed a coarse profanity. Fortunately, there were no pedestrians at that moment, for otherwise I am sure they would have returned the gesture.

Oxford was our first experience of cruising through an urban centre, past restaurants and under queues of traffic. The river split around an island and passing under Folly Bridge, I was confronted with a flotilla of racing eights and their crews. One of the boats was coming from the left and across my bow. Since I was in a narrow channel, I couldn't ease up on the throttle and wait for it to pass. Reluctantly, I honked the horn to make the crew aware. Muttering among themselves, they dipped their oars into the river and halted, allowing me to cruise out of the channel and past them. None of the crew returned my greeting and I guessed I had broken some taboo. Or they were just super focused. Whatever.

The river downstream of Folly bridge was a nice straight for the teams to practice on and I kept to the right, giving them their room while we enjoyed the spectacle they provided. We had never paid much attention to the sport and apart from the annual derby between Oxford and Cambridge, knew next to nothing about it. Cruising past the club houses was truly an eye-opener to the amount of money involved. The real estate the clubhouses occupy must be worth many millions and then there are the boats and all the associated running costs.

The day was magical, more so now that we were past Osney Bridge and the shadow it had thrown. We could now marvel at the farmland and meticulous estates that fronted the water. The slow and steady beat of the engine was quite hypnotic and, being a Sunday, our tummies began to demand food. On cue, a lock appeared ahead and right beside it was a majestic oak tree and English pub, Kings Arms. It was fate, and I was not going to question it.

Spotting a good bank, I eased Wyebourne around and brought her in close enough for my wife to hop out with the mooring line. After a satisfying lunch in the beautiful sunshine, we had a good hour's rest on our comfy beds before setting off for another few hours of cruising.

Abingdon came into sight and we gawked at the multitude of boat types moored along the river there. Very soon we exited the Oxfordshire town and came to Culham Cut, a canal that bypasses an unnavigable stretch of the Thames. It was now late afternoon and despite our after-lunch nap, we were beat. I was surprised at how much a day of cruising and traversing locks had tired us. We had estimated it would take five days to reach Devizes and I began to question if this was realistic. A likely looking spot to moor up for the night appeared on the cut and we quickly brought Weybourne in and tied her up.

As it was still light, I took a long walk, glad to be able to stretch my legs. Thirty minutes later, I discovered a hydro plant in nearby Culham using three large Archimedes Screws. I knew at once what the devices were. I had recently been researching notable characters from the Second Punic War for the Sons of Iberia series. One of them was Archimedes of Syracuse, the chap that ran down the street naked shouting, 'Eureka, Eureka'. He had visited Egypt and observed these water screws being used to transfer water from ditches to higher elevations. In Culham, the screws are turned by the natural flow of the Thames and this generates enough electricity to power 120 homes.

The following morning, we set off, hopeful we could reach Reading by late afternoon. The first clouds appeared just before lunch and rain soon threatened. Not prepared to travel in the rain, we moored up and raised the canopy over the stern deck. Half an hour later the dark clouds opened and rain began to fall for the rest of the afternoon. Shelving any thought of further travel, we spent a cosy afternoon sprucing up the interior of the boat. There were old tools, cans of screws, tins of paint, and assorted odds and ends stashed in ingenious little cupboards all over the boat. Taking stock of it all was the job of many days and I got stuck into that. I found it particularly useful to see what products were used on the boat in the past.

The clouds thinned and disappeared overnight to gift us a fresh morning. Eating breakfast on the rear deck, we watched as swans feasted on mayflies and begged for crumbs. It would be our last day on the Thames and we were in no rush as we set off. Arriving in Reading, we moored up so that we could walk into town and get a few groceries before turning onto the Kennet and Avon Canal.

CHAPTER 5
LOCKS AND LADDERS

The Kennet and Avon Canal. Going Medieval.

We had just got the hang of locks on the Thames when we arrived in Reading and turned onto the Kennet and Avon Canal. The first lock we arrived at was Blake's Lock and what a difference it was. No more electric paddles and well-balanced gates. These paddles were all manual and the lock gates heavy brutes. We had learned by now not to rush and took our time to make sure there were no accidents. Upriver from Blake's Lock, we reached a traffic light control. Yes, you read that right. We had to stop for a red light. We were required to press a button located on a post on the side of the canal. This would turn the lights red for boats coming in the opposite direction. This was necessary because the watercourse was confined between the building that rose up to either side and it was impossible to see oncoming vessels around the sharp corners.

Between my inexperience and the current, I could not get Wyebourne close enough to reach the button. In desperation, we called to a passing bloke and asked him to press it for us. He did so without changing expression and I wondered if this was a regular request? The light duly turned green and I eased Wyebourne forward and between the towering buildings of the city.

Exiting Reading, we had one more hurdle and it rated among our worst. Fobney Lock is a deep lock with the bottom gate set just upstream of a bridge. A steep weir empties water beneath the hanging lock landing while the river Kennet flows into the pond from the opposite side. With these conflicting currents at work on the hull, I had to edge up to the lock landing so that my wife could jump onto it. On my first attempt, I misjudged my approach and Wyebourne ricocheted sickeningly off the metal. There was nothing to do but circle around and try again, and I could only wonder at how folks managed seventy-foot narrowboats in such water. The second attempt did the trick and my wife hopped off Wyebourne, windlass in hand, to close the paddles and open the lock gates.

One thing about setting locks is the spectacle they offer curious tourists and holidaymakers. There was a young family at Fobney Lock when we went through and the father asked if he could film us managing the lock. He spent twenty minutes filming us and then took my WhatsApp details to send me the footage. Sure enough, a month later, I received a message from him with the footage attached.

Committed to pacing ourselves, we took the opportunity to have a rest after exiting the lock upriver. While relaxing in the sun, a couple came through the lock in a fifty-foot narrowboat and moored up behind us with a friendly wave. We began talking and I discovered that they had been boating on the country's waterways for many years and this was a first visit to the Kennet and Avon Canal. I was immeasurably relieved to find that they too had found the locks and bridges as challenging as we had. From here on, the canal became progressively more medieval.

That evening we arrived in Theale. Suitably armed with the correct key purchased from the Canal and River Trust, we opened our first swing bridge. Tying up on the visitor moorings just beyond the bridge, we decided to call a halt to our cruise. The physical aspect of setting multiple locks daily was taking its toll, especially on my wife who, to be fair, was doing the lion's share of the physical work. Since the aborted attempt at steering on the Thames, she refused to touch the boat wheel. So, while I manoeuvred Wyebourne, she was the one winding open the paddles and pushing open the lock gates. Added to the physical effort, was the emotional strain of the whole move and lifestyle change.

The result was that, although we had planned on cruising up to Devizes in Wiltshire, it was apparent that we needed a rest. The following day, it rained steadily most of the day. The slow drum of rain on the cabin roof was like being inside one of the ambient sound CDs. We were glad of our decision to remain on the visitor mooring for the day, relax, and take stock.

Examining our options, we decided to overhaul our entire plan. Instead of cruising on to Devizes, we'd only go as far as Ufton Nervet. There, we would find a likely spot and moor up for two weeks. A fortnight is the longest a boat may moor in one place on the waterways. The alternative is to rent an annual residential mooring along the canal or in a marina. These are not only costly, they are also hard to come by. We therefore planned to *Continuously Cruise*. This meant we'd need to move on at least every two weeks to a new spot. The upside was that we did not pay for mooring. The trick was to find places to moor where we could also park the car. In preparation, we had already scoped out the canal through the Vale of Pewsey in Wiltshire, where we expected to do most of our cruising. Here we had identified likely places to park near the canal. Now that we would not be going that far, I needed to do a reconnaissance of the canal around Ufton Nervet. This was as easy as calling up a satellite map of the area. In less than half an hour, I identified a potential place where we could park just off the canal. The test would be to see if we could moor there as well.

The following morning, we were rested but tense. This was the first test of how viable the continuous cruising option would be. We chugged along the Kennet river which forms the eastern length of the Kennet and Avon Canal, studying the shoreline. It was lined with a barbed wire fence and plenty of signs indicating residential mooring only. I did not particularly want to moor on the river, so this did not worry me too much. Reaching Ufton swing bridge, we passed through it onto a portion of man-made canal. Boats may only moor on the towpath side of the canal. As we cruised slowly west, I eyed the thick reeds growing between us and the towpath with trepidation. We were already past the place we would park the car and the reeds showed no sign of letting up. On a whim, I edged Wyebourne closer to the towpath, hoping not to foul the propeller. She slid closer and closer without mishap. When the hull scraped the canal bottom, there was just a few feet between the boat and the path. Our gangplank could easily bridge the distance. I throttled back and went into reverse until Wyebourne was stationary. Then, with mooring line in hand, I jumped onto the towpath.

We were two hundred yards from the swing bridge and there were no signs prohibiting mooring. It looked promising. My wife threw the mooring pins to me and after hammering them in and tying Wyebourne up, I hopped back onboard and laid the gangplank out. It just reached. It was also very springy. I had knocked it together using decking board and where before it had seemed ideal, now it looked too short, too narrow and not thick enough. I'd have to try again. In the meantime, we seemed to have found our first two week mooring. We looked at one another with cautious optimism. There were no other boats moored anywhere in sight and that worried me a little. Also, it would be a long commute to Swindon each day. We figured that since we would be moving further west along the canal every fortnight, we would slowly close the distance. By the time winter arrived, we would be in the vicinity of Great

Bedwyn, which was under twenty miles from Swindon.

Commuting was always going to be one of the aspects of this new life that we would need to adapt to. We had rarely commuted further than from one side of town to the other. Now we would have to commute from miles away in the country to our places of work. Not so much an issue in summer, but on the shortest days of winter, it would mean driving to and from work in the dark on country roads.

As it turned out, the mooring proved ideal. Especially after I knocked together a longer gangplank which has proved invaluable for mooring along the rough-and-ready banks of the Kennet and Avon Canal.

Our preparation for life onboard a boat, continuously cruising along the waterways of England, had largely been watching countless videos online. I remember sitting in our rented house, watching people effortlessly tie knots and the best and fastest way to tie a mooring line. We had also watched hours of videos on setting locks. Correctly setting a lock is not difficult, nor complicated. A lock is a construction which links one stretch of waterway with another stretch on a different level. In essence, it is an elevator. In this way, boats can cruise up or downhill. Wherever possible, the natural watercourse is used. Where a river becomes unnavigable, engineers build canals that bypass these stretches.

Our course from Reading was uphill, shadowing the watercourse of the Kennet River. As we approached a lock, I would steer close to the lock landing to allow my wife to hop out. She would then ensure the upstream paddles and gates were closed. The paddles are the sluice gates within the lock gate itself. She'd then open the lower gates and I'd steer Wyebourne into the lock and throw her the fore and aft mooring lines. She would wrap them around a bollard and pass them back to me on the boat. Once the bottom gates were closed, she would then open the paddles in the upper gates, one side at a time to allow water to flood the lock and lift Wyebourne to the higher level. When the water level in the lock was equal to the water level in the canal above the lock, my wife would then push each gate open. While the water was gushing into the lock, I would hang onto the mooring rope to keep Wyebourne from cracking against the lock walls in the turbulence. Our greatest fear was allowing the back end of the boat to get stuck on the cil of the lock, which can cause it to tip and flood. This is only a danger when going down a flight.

One of the things the first lock keeper we met on the Thames explained to us was how to flood the lock without causing the boat to be battered around. He explained that it was best to open the paddle on the side of the lock the boat was tied to. That way, the inrushing water would pin the boat to the side.

In practice, opening and closing a lock is like an obstacle course. We threw ropes, climbed ladders, and walk gingerly across beams with a long fall on one side and freezing water on the other. We needed to winch open paddles and then use our weight to open and close four lock gates weighing many tons each. The greatest lesson we learned was to pace ourselves and to never rush or do it when tired.

Every lock is unique. Some are shallow. Others have easy to swing gates. Then there is Monkey Marsh Lock. Built (dug) in 1723, it is one of only two remaining turf-sided locks and is a listed historic monument. In reality, it's a hole in the ground with a bunch of steel girders lining it and there is a reason there are only two left. No, I am not a fan. I love history, probably more than many, but there is a limit.

There are the locks where you have to walk all the way around to the other side using a brick and mortar bridge. Some locks have walkways attached to the gates. Others have pedestrian bridges across them. I clipped one of these bridges once with my mast light and scared the folk on it silly.

Naturally, as the day progressed and we reached lock five or six, we became tired and touchy. I'd grind my teeth with impatience as my wife trudged from paddle to paddle. She would give me killer stares if I allowed Wyebourne to drift in the lock. Once, I took the boat in further than usual and she panicked, thinking the water gushing into the lock from under the top gates would flood the boat. On another occasion, I noticed her edging across a lock gate in the rain. I dared not say a word in case I distracted her, causing her to slip and fall. When she reached the other side, I pointed to the bridge she could have used and she nearly threw the windlass at me.

Slowly, we became used to the locks and our confidence in our ability increased. I could help with the gates now that we knew how sturdy Wyebourne was and how to fill the locks without her tossing about. Eventually, I was happy to do the locks single-handedly. Later in the year, cruising between Hungerford and Froxfield, my wife went ahead in the car to meet me at a lock further up. I reached a swing bridge behind a church, aptly named Hungerford Church Swing Bridge, and found that I could not budge it. The Vicar, who was outside chatting to parishioners, noticed and came over to lend a shoulder for which I was eternally grateful. At the next lock, Hungerford Marsh Lock, I discovered that a swing bridge was set over the lock. A double whammy. Fortunately, this bridge was easier to shift and I set about tying off Wyebourne and closing the gates. I am not fond of heights and sidling between the bridge and the lock wasn't much fun, especially as it is one of the deeper locks. Falling into a lock would be bad enough if there was somebody around to fish you out. Falling in when alone is bad news, and so I was glad to put that lock behind me without mishap.

That was a day for struggles because the very next lock, Cobblers Lock, had wonky gates. My wife met me there and we set the lock while I told her about the Vicar and the swing bridge and lock combo. Fifteen minutes later, we were still waiting for the lock to fill enough to open the top gates. If the water in the lock is lower than the water above the lock, it's practically impossible to open the gates. Going around to the lower gates, I saw the problem at once. A huge rooster's tail of water was spraying from between the lower gates where they had not closed tight. This was preventing the lock from filling enough to open the top gates. We had to drain the lock and close the lower gates again, this time making sure we slammed them tight to seal them and prevent water from spraying out.

To date, the record number of locks we have set in a day is twelve. We started off below Wootton Rivers and finished upstream from Beech Grove Lock near Great Bedwyn. This stretch of the Kennet and Avon Canal climbs out of the Vale of Pewsey to Crofton, where the Crofton Beam Engine is situated, and then descends to Great Bedwyn. Nothing as steep as the Caen Hill flight in Devizes, it nevertheless offers a rigorous workout and by the last, I was pretty much staggering.

As we came down the flight, a wide beam barge came up out of a lock. This thing was a behemoth and I put Wyebourne over to the right as far as I dared, only for the barge to drag her back towards it. At the last minute, I managed to fend Wyebourne off the barge with my foot, narrowly avoiding cracking their lowered cockpit windows. Dirty looks duly exchanged, I carried on down the flight to discover a tiny *yoghurt pot* partially submerged. The stretch of water between one lock and the next is called a pound. I am not sure why. I would have called it a pond perhaps, but there we go. This flight is notorious for rapidly changing water levels and either flooding or emptying. Either is bad news for boats moored there as it will tip and allow water in through loose *skin fittings* or over the *gunwale*. I was to learn this valuable lesson first-hand the following day.

Shattered and thirsty, we finally moored up. The only reason we had pushed so hard was because Canal and River Trust (CRT) had been struggling all summer to keep the water levels up in the pounds and were chaining the lock gates closed in the middle of the afternoon. Since it was late and the gates were to be chained shortly, I moored up for the night on the lock landing below lock 62. It was a beautiful late summer evening and the birdsong gradually gave way to the flitting of bats. We slept like a pair of logs that night and rose stiff as boards the next morning. I had found a great place to moor up for the next two weeks, and because it was just above lock 63, we did not need to go through another lock. Ten minutes later, I had Wyebourne up against the bank, mooring ropes secured to pins. It was a beautiful morning and we set off to walk back up to Wootton Rivers to fetch our car. It was a leisurely three-hour walk and I amused myself by foraging for cobnuts. On returning, the moment I spotted Wyebourne, I went cold. The boat was listing badly to starboard, the mooring lines as taut as bowstrings. I raced down the towpath and as I did; I noticed that the water level in the pound had dropped by a good two feet. Stepping onto Wyebourne, I immediately felt the hull crunch into the canal bed. I untied the mooring lines and cursed when I noticed the centre cleat had snapped off. I started up the engine and while it was idling; I tried to refloat Wyebourne by pushing off with the gangplank. I used every trick I had learned, but it was impossible and there wasn't a Vicar to be seen. I did not want to use the engine to drive her off the mud as there was a good chance of breaking or bending the propeller blades. In this instance, I had no choice and I throttled forward slowly. The prop clipped a few stones, but the hull was too grounded to move. Guessing where it was sticking, I got my wife to hang off the starboard side bow rail and this just managed to lift the hull enough to get us clear of the mud. If we had stopped off to do some shopping or taken just a little longer to return to Wyebourne, we may very well have found our home half-filled with water.

The lesson I learned that day was never to moor on short pounds where there is a chance the water level can fall and strand your boat. There is also a case for not tying the mooring lines so tight that they snap the cleats when the boat drops with the water level.

CHAPTER 6
THE BOATING COMMUNITY

Old salts, solitary boaters, and boating families. Hire boaters and locals. The towpath hikers, canoeists and the fishing addicts.

Leaving behind life in a rented house in a large town also meant leaving behind a stereotypical nosey neighbour. Goodbye to the little white Maltese Poodle next door, whose constant yapping bark worked its way through two sets of double glazing and into the very fabric of your consciousness. Left behind were the pizza delivery drivers who were forever mistaking our house for one on a different road. No more clinking of bottles and rumble of wheelie bins on rainy Tuesday mornings either. The banshee wailing of emergency response vehicle sirens was replaced by a chorus of cooing doves and chirruping robins. The cityscape exchanged for a revolving palette of countryside scenes, passing boaters, pedalling cyclists and rambling hikers.

Our first boat neighbour was a pleasure boater in a gleaming white thirty-foot cabin cruiser with matching red fenders and canopy. We nodded cordially to one another across the river as he hauled buckets of water out of the

Thames to rinse and wash his pride and joy every other day. This manner of greeting was to set the pattern for our interactions with most boaters in the coming months and years.

While moored at Radcot in May, two fellows arrived up the towpath to settle down against the fence where they could soak up the sun. They soon cracked open a can of store-bought lager each, and catching my eye, one of them raised his can to me. He ambled over to the boat and began a conversation, expressing a lot of interest in Wyebourne. Since we were not yet living permanently onboard, my ingrained towny fear of theft kicked in and I kept my answers deliberately vague. Over the coming months, I was to discover how deeply this mistrust of strangers was ingrained into me. In time, living alongside busy towpaths and canals has gone a long way to relieving me of this burden.

Since the May weather was warm and sunny, there was a steady stream of people out for the day, passing right beside the boat. This might sound like a nightmare for an introvert like myself, but people going for walks beside the river on such days are usually bright and cheerful. It would take an especially sour person, our bitter old ex-neighbour for instance, not to feel uplifted in such company.

On our voyage down the Thames, we quickly discovered the diverse nature of our fellow boaters. While there was a minority that looked away rather than exchange a nod, most would happily wave. There was, of course, the bloke with the pink mohawk on a narrow boat draped with camouflage netting who took a shine to my wife from across the river and loudly invited her to join him. What? And I was chopped liver?

During the winter of 2018/19, a narrowboat moored up behind us on our winter mooring spot. It was two days before I even saw the bloke who lived on it and another day before we encountered one another outside. A retired train driver from up north, he had bought his boat years before and had cruised the length and breadth of the country's waterways. The tiny village we were moored in had exactly zero shops and one pub, which was open for four hours in the evenings. Our neighbour had no car and although he did not ask, I offered to take him up to Marlborough to buy any groceries he needed. He smiled broadly and happily accepted my invitation, remarking that he had never encountered such a sleepy village. As evidence that neither he nor I talk much, it was only during the short four-mile car journey that I learned his name and a little more about his life and boating experiences.

What were you doing when you first realised how you unconsciously label people? I know that I was cleaning cobwebs from the canopy over the deck of Wyebourne in the late summer sun outside Newbury. We had been in place for a day when a tall bloke walked past with an open can of beer in hand and a rottweiler at his heels. I eyed him sceptically as he crossed the swing bridge and went off to wherever he was going. I am not sure why, but I immediately distrusted him. Was it the open beer can? The deeply tanned face and knotted ponytail? His stern look? What changed my perception of him? Again, nothing specific.

He would nod to us as he passed on the way to his boat, which he lived onboard with a partner who was a little more outgoing, offering a smile when she passed. One afternoon, I heard someone hacking wood nearby and looking out, saw the bloke wielding a machete. He was chopping the woody vines stems that were wrapped around a tree that grew off the towpath. He passed the boat and started on another tree, cutting through the vine quickly before looking longingly over the fence at the trees growing there. Entry was prohibited to everyone except members of a local fishing club. Turning around, he caught my eye and with a shrug and wry smile, he said, "I don't expect the fishermen would like me over there." We grinned in solidarity for a moment, recognising a mutual disdain for people that fence off the land for their own pleasure. When I told my wife about this encounter later, I jokingly referred to the bloke as Jungle George and his partner became Xenia. Hacking the vine stems stops them from strangling and killing the trees around which they grow. Nothing scares a boater quite like a large tree weakened by vines swaying drunkenly in the wind. We never progressed beyond nodded greetings, and to us, they remained Jungle George and Xenia. A few months later, my son was helping me move Wyebourne over the summit at Crofton and down to our winter mooring in the Vale of Pewsey. As we cruised along, I spied their boat moored along the towpath and told my son this was the bloke we had spoken of. The dog appeared on the deck to give us the beady eye and sure enough, Jungle George appeared after it. I nodded a greeting in the established fashion, but my son waved and shouted, "Hi, George!" This earned him a very confused look from the bloke while I had to choke back my laughter.

Boaters have their cliques too. Some are more than that though and we encountered three boaters who had become firm friends, a tribe almost, who stayed together as they cruised. Over the summer of 2018, we were moored near them on two occasions. One boat belonged to a couple with five children, four of them no older than ten. I never heard them bickering or complaining, and on weekends and after school, they were always out on the towpath, playing and laughing. What a wonderful way to spend their childhood days as opposed to being addicted to computer games and smart phones.

Another of the group came around one evening to introduce himself. Since I was about to barbeque some steaks, we invited him to eat with us and in no time, we were sitting around the fire together having a meal. I will never forget the surprise I experienced when, as the night grew darker, he reached into his inner coat pocket and pulled out a tiny spirit lamp which he then lit and set on the table. To this day I wonder what else he kept in those pockets? A sewing kit? Duct tape? A bulldog clip at least!

It was early September and during our conversation he innocently asked how we would be heating the boat through winter. When I replied that we were still thinking about it, he shook his head and warned us that we did not have much longer before the first frost. It was true, and I really needed to make a plan. In his experience, we could survive a winter on the boat without heating, but it would be utterly miserable, and we would quickly come to hate it.

We also met a pair of boaters that travelled together on individual boats. Friends only, they were younger than the average boaters we have met. We got to know them when she came over to alert me that our mooring pins had come loose after a boat had gone past at well over the 4mph speed limit. I was happy to repay that friendly warning when I noticed she had left her car headlights on one night.

In our experience, most liveaboard boaters are lone men, and predominantly late middle age or older. Many have been boating for years and are deeply rooted in the boating community. While I have no doubt that there is an element of loneliness in their lives, I think that for the most part, they enjoy their solitary existence, happy to avoid socialising and large groups. There are a few women boaters who live alone, also mostly older women and we met one lady who I recognised from her social media profile on a boater group.

Despite the semi-solitary nature of most boaters, there is a genuine spirit of community welfare among them that is extended to the people that live in the villages along the waterways and even to the visitors that use the towpaths and canals for recreation.

When we originally planned where we would moor, we estimated we would cruise between Newbury in the east, and Devizes in the west. The voyage down the Thames and up the Kennet and Avon Canal proved to be more exhausting than we had expected, and at Theale we decided to moor up for two weeks at the next spot we could find. This proved to be two hundred yards west of the Ufton

Nervet swing bridge. There was a small area off the road where we could park our car and the walk to the boat was no more than a couple of minutes. We later learned that there had been a horrific rail accident at the adjacent rail crossing in 2004. At the time, it had been a level crossing and one November evening, the London Paddington to Plymouth service collided with a car parked on the rails. The collision caused the entire train to derail and claimed the lives of seven people with twelve more seriously injured. The level crossing was replaced with a road bridge in 2016, twelve years later.

It was the last weekend of May and the first hire boaters were beginning to take to the waterways. In the days that followed, we watched with increasing nerves as the occasional novice battled to steer past Wyebourne. On one occasion, I was forced to shout a warning to a distracted fellow who veered past my stern, missing us by under a foot. He grinned cheekily at me as he passed and commented that there was plenty of space.

There is an element of wariness about hire boaters among the resident liveaboard community. Over the summer, the peak period for hire boat companies, social media groups are abuzz with reports of irresponsible and reckless behaviour by hire boaters. As always, it is only a tiny minority of people that behave badly and cause most of the grief. These seem to nearly always be groups of blokes on benders. Misbehaviour includes, speeding, partying into the early hours of the morning, throwing beer cans overboard and abusive language directed at passers-by and other boaters. In one extreme incident in 2019, a hire boat party was accused of causing the sinking of a wooden narrowboat and the loss of a vulnerable pensioner's only home.

Our experience of hire boaters has always been pleasant. It is lovely to see the joy on people's faces as they soak up the beauty of the canal and experience life on a boat.

Other frequent users of the canal are canoeists. We spent our first winter moored up at Wootton Rivers and arriving back one Tuesday, discovered the car park full and pairs of neoprene clad canoeists paddling up and down the canal in the dark. They were training for the annual Devizes to Westminster canoe race that takes place over the Easter weekend. We happened to be moored at Pewsey when the race took place in 2019 and had front row seats to the hundreds of canoeists that paddled past. It was a fine sunny Saturday morning and I sat out on the front of the boat to watch. I was impressed in particular by the front runner, who hardly seemed to be putting any effort into paddling and yet was zooming along. The resident pair of swans were far less enthusiastic about the race than us human spectators. I'll admit that it was rather entertaining to see canoeists scatter at the sight of the large cob heading for them, hissing and posturing with his wings.

While mooring between Ufton Nervet outside Reading and Newbury, we were amazed at how busy the towpath was and how many people use it to commute to work. From the crack of dawn to well after sunset, cyclists were up and down outside our windows. What a great resource to get to work and I can imagine that together with the exercise, the views and fresh air would make for a very productive start to the working day.

Two of the more out-of-the-ordinary visitors we encountered were a group of women paddle boarders strung out across the width of the Thames and the remnants of a pool party held on the Kennet River. When I saw the paddle boarders, I naturally goggled in surprise and respectfully slowed right down. Since then, Standup Paddleboarding (SUP) has become one of the fastest growing watersports in the UK. Unlike canoes, these do not create much of a wash and are virtually silent. On more than a couple of occasions, I've been talking away to myself in the galley and looked up in time to see people gliding past the window with bemused expressions.

The pool party happened while I was out, and I can only imagine the fun had. I know it happened because when I returned to the boat, there was what can only be described as an inflatable table and seats for four people discarded under the bridge and the empty cans of obligatory supermarket lager scattered about.

While moored outside Woolhampton, during the height of the scorching 2018 summer, I marvelled at the constant stream of hikers that passed along the towpath. Again, they appeared at all hours of the day and often in large groups. One party of at least thirty or more strolled past over the course of five minutes, every one of them well over pensionable age. I don't know where they started from, but none of them had water bottles or hats and the weather was like a furnace.

The fishing enthusiasts are also a constant source of interest with their poles, wheelbarrows and tackle boxes. At the outset of life as an off-grid boater, my heart would sink whenever I cruised around a bend to discover fishermen and women sitting along the towpath, poles extended across the width of the canal. As I cruised closer, they'd all patiently retract their poles until I had passed. Over winter, pike fishing is the rage and the enthusiasts descend on the canal from early in the morning on the weekends. There is something quite disconcerting about stumbling off the boat in a quiet spot far from anywhere only to discover a stranger standing behind the boat casting for pike. I immediately begin replaying the last ten minutes in my mind, wondering what he might have overheard.

They do not limit their fishing expeditions to the weekends either, as I discovered. We had attracted the custom of a pair of swans and their two almost adult offspring, who were forever knocking on the hull for handouts. One morning, as I sat working on my laptop, the swans arrived and as usual, I tossed a few handfuls of bran flakes out for them. They usually leave us alone for a few hours after being fed, but not ten minutes later, I heard them pecking at the front of the boat. I slid open the window and told them in no uncertain terms to bugger off before slamming the window shut. As I closed it, I spotted a pike fisherman slinking away, thoroughly confused, no doubt, as to why I had told him to get lost.

The reason I think they like to fish so close to the boat is because the pike and perch are attracted to the boat's shadows. From the shadow of the boat, these predators can launch attacks on the shoals of fingerlings that pass. The fishermen try to get their spinners to pass beside the boat to lure out the big one. In windy conditions, the lures sometimes clatter off the boat and I have discovered a spinner hooked into the mooring line where it attaches to the cleat. I expect when I haul Wyebourne out of the water for a repaint, I'll find an assortment of fishing lures dangling from the prop and rudder.

Relations between residents along the canal and boaters vary from confrontational to community spirited. I try to steer clear of any unpleasantness by respecting people's property and their environment. The only grievance I have had with a local resident occurred one autumn. It was in a little village where the average property price is nearly £600,000. We moored up outside the village in a sunny spot opposite a forest and strip of grassed land. We had been there for a week when a vehicle arrived on the property opposite us with a trailer of garden waste. The driver tipped out the grass cuttings, leaves and branches and after dousing it with petrol, set it ablaze. Being fairly green, it smouldered for much of the day rather than burn up. The following day, I was on the front of the boat, sanding and painting the upper hull when he arrived with another load. Accompanying him was an elderly man who was clearly the property owner. Seeing me watching, he gestured up the canal and asked me to move along to avoid the smoke. As a local, he would have known that I would have to move at least a mile due to mooring restrictions his town have imposed along the canal. I declined to move and went about my business. Unfortunately, the breeze shifted later that day and the main column of smoke drifted over Wyebourne. In an age when the climate crisis is a known and accepted fact, it still baffles me that landowners find it necessary to burn fallen leaves and garden waste. Especially when their properties are so vast they could easily build compost heaps that would add beneficial nutrients to their soil. I did move. I had no choice when a woman arrived in the dark with a torch that night to add still more waste to the smouldering pile. The smoke grew so thick that it set off the smoke alarm on Wyebourne and by morning my sinuses were swollen. I have no doubt that I would have had a visit from local authorities had it been my smoke drifting through the landowner's bedroom. Other than that occasion, interactions with village and town residents have been positive and I am happy to spend money at local restaurants, grocers, and businesses.

CHAPTER 7
SUMMER CRUISING

Early sunrises, sunshine, and umbrellas. Buzzing solar panels and overflowing battery banks. Emptying the porta potty. The wildlife. The stars. Our first stowaway. Me-me-me.

Cruising along the waterways and living onboard our boat during summers is a real pleasure. We had lived in Swindon ever since arriving in the UK. While we knew the weather further east was warmer, we had never really grasped the difference a matter of thirty miles could make. We would wake to green trees and birdsong, all backlit by brilliant blue skies. An hour later, commuting west along the M4, we'd crest the summit of the hills a few miles outside of Swindon to find it obscured under a thick bank of fog. It was at moments like those that I wanted to kick myself for not making the move sooner.

Cruising down the Thames on those first few days, we encountered a swan with a string of fuzzy grey cygnets towing along behind her. While eyeing the near riverbank for a convenient spot to moor, I watched the swan continue its course to intercept the boat. I recalled when we were onboard the hire boat the previous September that a pair of swans had nonchalantly allowed the boat's bow wake to ease them aside. I thought the same would happen if this family came too close. Sure enough, the mother and her chicks disappeared from my sight as they approached the front of the boat. A heartbeat later, the mother swan appeared alongside the stern of the boat with her chicks. Minus three. While I was still counting them, two of the missing chicks popped up from under the water in the wake of the boat. Eyes goggling, I quickly slammed the throttle into neutral. At this, the last cygnet shot out of the wake, chirruping indignantly. Evidently, the chicks had been sucked under the boat. I was horrified at what could have happened had they encountered the propeller. That evening, the mother swan and her brood arrived alongside the boat where we had moored, and accompanying them was the father. The moment I saw him, he gave me a menacing hiss and I felt the weight of accusation in his beady stare. Feeling compelled to apologise and make restitution, I dropped him and his family a good few slices of wholewheat bread.

While moored at Ufton Nervet, the warm spring weather developed into thunderstorms worthy of movies of Armageddon. One lunchtime, while alone on Wyebourne and writing the third book in a series, the sky abruptly grew dark and a sharp wind kicked up. I raced to lift the pram top, the canopy over the rear deck, and as I was clipping it into place, lightening strobed across the angry clouds. Two seconds later, a thunderclap rocked me on heels and the heavens opened. At first, I was enthralled. I have always loved thunderstorms and rain. Then I remembered the two gas cylinders plumbed into the boat's gas lines and I felt a little queasy. I hurried to close the cylinders, unsure what might happen if a bolt of lightning struck the boat. To the left, a forest of tall poplar trees lined the bank of the canal and I winced at the thought of lightening hitting them and spraying wood splinters all over the boat. Okay, I admit it; I have a vivid imagination. My solution to my increasing nerves was to sit on the gas box. I reasoned that if the boat was struck and the cylinders exploded, I would not feel a thing.

Those poplar trees were the favoured roost of a murder of crows. You know how they got that collective noun? They murdered someone with the sheer volume of caw-cawing they made. Between the crows and the threat of falling branches, I vowed to avoid mooring beneath such lofty boughs in the future. The thunderstorms were not over yet either. One evening after we'd eaten a fresh salad for dinner and were watching the ever-circling terns feasting on mayflies, a huge thunderhead developed to the east. From within the dark mass, electric blue lightning flickered. It was better viewing than any Guy Fawkes fireworks, and the oddest thing was that we heard not the faintest sound of thunder since the wind was blowing from the west.

Ufton Nervet was the last place we saw the terns. Just a mile to the west, they were replaced by swallows who soared down the length of the canal and performed aerial acrobatics high above the boat. Early mornings were alive with the gentle chirping of tits and peering through the skylight above our beds, we watched as long-tail tits flitted from twig to twig.

One hot Saturday afternoon near Padstow, my wife happened to glance over her shoulder in time to spot a creature swimming across the canal. We jumped to our feet for a better look and I was surprised to see that it was a snake. I could not tell if it was an adder or harmless grass snake, and in seconds it slid into the vegetation beside the towpath. I have not seen another snake since.

I spend a lot of time on my laptop, researching and writing historical fiction set in ancient Spain and take regular breaks off the boat to stretch my legs. In high summer, I will often go walking at sunset, revelling in the twilight hour. Not only does this increase my step count, the fresh air also helps me think up new plots, story arcs and character development for my books. Out at twilight in rolling fields of coppery summer wheat, my mind will wander off as I stare entranced at the hazy scenery. Imagine then my fright, when one evening, as the last light faded to dark, the silence was shattered by the thundering charge of a dark shape tearing along the very path I stood on. Stumbling backwards, I yelled aloud as a surprised badger did a smart about turn and raced off. I'm a slow learner. Not a week later, lost in thought as I strolled back to the boat, a galloping hare almost collided with me. On the hard-packed ground, it sounded as large as a horse and its speed was phenomenal as it careened towards me, tearing me from whatever daydream I had been enjoying. If I could have caught my breath, I might have screamed like a girl. As it was, the best I could muster was to clap my hands in fright. Hard to believe that thirty years earlier, I used to lay awake listening to predators circle our bush camps. When I say predators, I do not mean foxes and stoats. I mean African lions and spotted hyenas.

The animals we encounter in our life as off-grid boaters are not always wild. Domestic cats and dogs are common pets among boaters and cats especially, being curious beasts by nature, will come visiting. We were moored on the Kennet outside Woolhampton, enjoying a visit from our son. It was another scorcher and a swan had lazily drifted nearer on the off chance of a free bite. The three of us were sitting looking over the rear bench at it when I felt a presence at my elbow. Turning, I found myself staring at a very confident cat perched beside me. He did not even acknowledge me, preferring to give the swan a thoroughly judgmental stare instead.

When he did deign to greet us and I reached to stroke him, a cloud of dust erupted from his fur. Gagging, I shooed him off the deck, but he was made of sterner stuff than that. He sprang onto the instrument panel and proceeded to groom himself while us humans hovered at his paws. In no time, he was off again and doing a complete inspection of Wyebourne, inside and out. We christened him Catos, after the protagonist in the Sons of Iberia series, and he came often to visit, although we refused to allow him into the cabins after his first dusty inspection.

No cat is stopped by mere humans though, and because it was 2018 and the summer was blistering hot, we slept with the aft cabin door open. I woke up on more than one occasion upon hearing stealthy paws landing on the bottom step. At half six every morning, Catos would take a walk around the outside of the boat, waking me with his mewling. For a little fun, I'd slide open my window a sliver and tease him with a bookmark. I've seen a lot of feral cats in my time, but none of them came close to his speed. In a flash, he'd leap, swiping it from my grip with his absolutely massive paws and fearsome claws.

I was sweltering on the rear deck one evening, a book in hand, when I noticed movement in the long grass beside the boat. Looking up, I saw Catos heading towards me, head low and shoulders high, much like a panther. Leaping from five feet away, he landed on the seat behind me in the usual cloud of red dust that immediately had my sinuses protesting. The worst was the large kill clenched firmly between his feline incisors. With a self-satisfied meow, he dropped the still-warm body of a kit at my feet. Naturally, I did what any other witness to murder would do. I grabbed my phone and took pictures. This must have offended Catos, because he reclaimed his gift to me and began to gnaw on it. That shook me. So, risking my fingers, I grabbed the poor dead bunny's back foot and tossed it into the dry grass on the riverbank. Catos fixed me with a withering stare before springing into the grass after his dinner. Over the next ten minutes, he devoured every last scrap of the creature.

I think it was after spurning his gift of freshly killed innocence that he planned his attack. And the esteemed SAS could not have planned and executed it with more stealth and cunning. Every evening, I'd turn off the gas and zip up the canopy doors. To prevent the canvas flapping, I would reach beneath the doors to secure the rubber loops. This was my usual routine just before bed. At this point in the night, I'm already half asleep. On the evening of the ambush, I went through all the usual motions of zipping up and then reaching beneath the canvas to secure the rubber loops. That was when he struck. Just as I reached into the dark with my face pressed up tight against the canopy. He sprang from out of the night to body slam the canvas right by my face. Caught totally unawares, I very nearly fell on my rear end in fright. Cursing like a sailor, I staggered upright to spend another ten minutes trying to secure the loops while avoiding his claws.

This was not the last surprise Catos had in store for us. On the evening of our wedding anniversary, we went out to enjoy a quiet, romantic dinner. After a delicious meal and feeling quite mellow, we strolled arm-in-arm back to Wyebourne, enjoying the balmy summer evening. Being a gentleman, I helped my wife onto the deck of Wyebourne before following her. As I did, she clenched my arm, her face pale, and pointed with a shaking hand at the ghastly object laying in the centre of the deck. I knew at once what I was looking at. There, in a drying pool of blood, was a rabbit's gallbladder.

The following day a silver-haired boater gave me a wave as he passed to moor upstream from Wyebourne. Soon after, he and a younger fellow with him began to refit some panelling inside their boat. Power tools humming and measuring tapes snapping; it sounded like all was going swimmingly until the older fellow tried to fit one of the newly cut panels. Muttered grumbling quickly grew into some very blue language which had us in hysterics. With a final, "For f***'sakes, Bob!" the silver-haired fellow erupted from the rear of the narrowboat and stormed off. When he returned half an hour later, he was in a much better mood and cradled in his arms, was none other than Catos, eyelids half-closed as his tummy was rubbed. As the fellow passed, Catos opened an eye to give me a smug stare.

There is a lot of debate about feeding wildlife. Many

parks in England discourage people from feeding bread to waterfowl, as apparently it is not healthy for them. After a big campaign to this effect, the advice was revised and people were told that a small amount of bread was not harmful to ducks and swans. For our part, and for different reasons, we try not to feed the wildlife from the boat. Not always successfully since I find it hard to deny the hopeful looks of mother duck and her brood.

The first winter onboard, I purchased a bird feeder that fitted to the outside of the window with suction pads. I had high hopes of photographing wild birds from inside the boat as they fed. Sure enough, the Blue Tits and Chaffinches quickly spotted the birdseed and got stuck in. I managed to snap a few blurry pics of them and hoped that the goldfinch would also join the party. They may have, but not while I was watching. No, what did come to dinner later that night was altogether less welcome. I had just put my head down and was a deep breath away from sleep when I heard a scrabbling sound. Tensing, I listened as the scrabbling turned to scratching. Rolling out of bed, I eased back the galley curtain and shone my torch into the bird feeder. Sure enough, a large rat, scaly tail and all, had squeezed his body into the feeder and was having a feast. The feeder came down the very next morning and the birds had to pick their seed from the towpath after that. The thing with rats is they get everywhere and, like all wildlife, the moment they discover an easy source of food, they keep returning. This is bad news as not only do they tend to gnaw on boat parts like electrical wires, they also spread a nasty disease called Weil's Disease.

Before our no-feeding animals and birds from the boat policy, I was happy to feed a pair of swans and their single surviving cygnet as they passed us twice a day. This was the pair that had nested near Pewsey and they had started off with a brood of six hatchlings. Between dog attacks and misadventure, the six sadly became one. I began to feed them fresh corn, slicing it off the cob so that the parents and the cygnet could strain it from the water in their natural feeding style. One evening, I accidentally dropped the fuzzy brown tassel from a fresh cob into the water between the swans where it floated, for all the world like a large brunette wig. Backpedalling frantically, the parents hissed at the fuzz, convinced it was a threat. The cygnet had other ideas and quickly slurped it up. The next time I fed them, I deliberately threw the fuzzy stuff in first and the parents were quick to try it too. Thereafter, they seemed to develop quite a taste for the stuff.

We christened the cygnet, Me-Me-Me after its habit of barging between its long-suffering parents, chirping what sounded like me-me-me at the top of its voice. While the parents looked on, it'd then devour the lion's share of the corn or bran flakes.

The elusive kingfisher is always a spectacular sight. If you are fast enough to look around when you hear its distinctive whistle. An incredibly shy bird; the most I usually manage to see is a flash of iridescent blue as it darts like a bullet away down the canal. One evening in the summer of 2020, I heard a soft scuffling on the canopy above the rear deck and guessed a bird had landed there. A few minutes later, a soft plop sounded in the canal behind the boat and the next moment a kingfisher darted past, not an arm's length from my face. I did not see a fish in its beak, but it returned every morning and evening after that so it must have been enjoying success catching its meals from there. I'd have liked nothing better than to get a photo of it, but it was way too wary and the moment I tried to peer out, it would shoot off. The closest I got to getting a photo was when I least expected to. I was sitting up in bed, sipping a cup of coffee and watching the rain slide endlessly down the windows when, with a flash of russet and blue, it alighted on the bow rail right outside my window. Thanks to the rain, all I managed to capture were two seconds of grainy movement.

CHAPTER 8
CREATURE COMFORTS

A good bed makes life great. Cold beers and crispy salads. Staying connected with mobile data. Thermal curtains and diesel heaters.

What do we miss most from living in a house? Perhaps a nice hot bath after getting soaked to the skin in the rain. Possibly hanging space for our clothes. Mostly, it is not worrying if I'll have enough electricity to power the heater, run our laptops, and charge our phones.

I'll describe these two facets of boatlife for those not familiar with the restrictions. First off, yes, we have a chemical toilet onboard Wyebourne. It is not the most spacious cubicle I've ever tried to turn around in, but it is there for our needs. The loo itself is called a *porta potty* and looks a lot like a passenger aircraft toilet. Waste is 'flushed' through a trapdoor into a small cassette which holds a detergent that breaks down solid matter and toilet paper. Twice a week, I remove the cassette and empty it at the nearest Canal and River Trust elsan facility.

Wyebourne was only used for short pleasure jaunts by the previous owners. I don't recall what I said when I was viewing her, but it made him scoff at the idea of living full time onboard the boat. I decided not to divulge that we intended to do just that. To power the electrics on the boat, it had a single leisure battery coupled up to the starter battery. As a nod to renewable energy, a solar panel the size of a dinner plate was connected to the electrics to trickle charge power into the batteries. The leisure battery was expected to power the lights wired into the boat as well as the water pump to the kitchen tap, the shower pump and the bilge pump. There was also an old tape cassette player and speakers wired into the power. Lastly, there was a single 12V outlet for running small electrical devices such as a cool box or an inverter. Hot water is generated by running the 2.9L diesel engine, which heats a calorifier and is plumbed into the shower and kitchen sink.

For our purposes, this was all adequate, especially over summer. For winter we needed heating and I was badly behind the curve on this by September. Our first inclination was to install a solid fuel burner. I did some online research and it all looked quite feasible. I had also seen plenty of cabin cruisers with tell-tale metal flues protruding from out of their cabin roofs, which brings me to one of my biggest reservations about a wood burner; cutting a new hole in a watertight roof. This was not something I was at all keen on doing, as leaks can develop so easily. I was fortunate enough to pop into a specialist supplier one day, just as one of their trade customers was there. The bloke heard me enquiring about wood burners and flues for fitting onboard a boat. Going out of his way, he put me in touch with a consultant at HETAS, the organisation that sets the Boat Safety Scheme standards for solid fuel burners on boats. It quickly became apparent that the configuration of the inside of Wyebourne would have to be changed to accommodate a wood burner safely. We would also need a lot more ventilation to be able to use it without risking carbon monoxide poisoning. As much as a little wood burner appealed, we decided against it.

What I chose to do next is a textbook example of false

economy. It seemed that every other boater ran a power generator and so I thought that would be the answer. I'd buy a good generator and use that to run a compatible fan heater as well as power anything else we needed to. I was confident that with the right generator and correct size heater, we'd be fine. I duly purchased one along with a fan heater that matched its continuous power output. I should add that it was now early November and nights were already long if not yet freezing. The generator proved to be a beast and truly noisy while the tiny fan heater was pitiful. It would barely heat the main cabin, let alone the rest of the boat. Every day proved to be colder than the next and in desperation, I purchased a small electric oil heater to see if that might be better able to warm us. It was not.

Thankfully, one day in early December, the generator refused to start. I removed and cleaned the spark plug, but that made no difference. I tried a new spark plug. Still no joy. I changed the oil and cleaned the air filter. Nothing worked.

It had been nearly a week and we had nothing but hot water bottles to keep us warm. I contacted the seller and jumped through the hoops needed to get my money back, including sharing a video of me trying to start the generator. In the meantime, I had been reading about the diesel heaters that are installed in trucks to keep the cabs warm while the driver catches up on his sleep. The original makes from Germany are exorbitantly expensive, but for a couple hundred quid, I could get a Chinese make. There were a variety of prices and sceptical of the ridiculously cheap ones, I took the plunge and ordered a moderately priced make with plenty of favourable reviews. It arrived a week later and was as easy to assemble as the videos had promised. The only thing I needed to supply was a charged leisure battery and ducting to deliver the warm air. With it connected and ready to go, I hit the on-switch and watched in apprehension as it hummed into life. It came with an LCD so I could watch as the temperature indication bars climbed from green to yellow to red and blisteringly hot air billowed out. It was fantastic. Best of all, the little contraption's fan was powerful enough to deliver super-hot air all the way from the stern to the front cabin, which is our bedroom.

The only downside was the heater draws a lot of power for a few minutes as it warms and I only had the one leisure battery. The solution was to install another battery and a solar panel.

Our first winter introduced us to another overlooked facet of boat life. Condensation. I had spent hours over summer, scrapping and filling hairline cracks in the gelcoat on the cabin roof. At times I thought I'd lost my vision from working on the blindingly white surface in the sun. All so that when winter came, there would be no water ingress into our living space. Little did I know that the traitors would be inside the boat. By traitors, I mean our lungs. The average human breathes out about two litres of water a day. Double that and factor in steam from cooking and you very quickly have a litre of water coating the inside of the boat. The most common advice given to combat condensation is to have plenty of ventilation. That might be fine in summer, but in the icy grip of winter, the last thing we wanted was to lose all our warm air to a breeze.

Thanks to my bumbling attempts to warm us and our boat, the condensation had gotten out of hand despite us wiping it dry every single day. At night we'd dry the cabin windows before wrapping ourselves in our duvets and in the morning, we'd wake to ice covered windows. Only, unlike a house, this ice was on the inside of the glass. On more than one occasion, I woke up to find a film of ice formed by my breath on the duvet. On those weekend mornings when we slept late, we'd wake up to the drip-drip-drip of melting ice falling onto our bedding and even off the roof into our faces. We laugh now at the green spot that blossomed on the ceiling right above our heads in those winter months. This was not some hideous growth, but the result of an old brass screw which has oxidised and caused the discolouration.

Hard on the heels of the condensation came another boating no-no. Mould. The ceiling of our boat very quickly became discoloured by mould, which is a serious health risk. Again, it was all we could do to treat it superficially, scrubbing it away and wiping the ceiling, walls and windows down twice a day. I bought a bag of cat litter, which is supposed to absorb water. Next, I tried a cheap plastic dehumidifier which uses a brick of some purple chemical to draw water out of the atmosphere. I didn't know it at the time, but the chemical is toxic. It certainly collected water in its little reservoir, but from the amount of condensation on every surface, you'd never have guessed it.

The diesel heater kept us warm though and got us through that first winter so we were able to take stock and adjust. With the ceiling cleaned and dry, we coated it with anti-mould paint and having gained a better understanding of the diesel heater, we could run it for much longer when winter came around again. The hot, dry air it generates is ideal for drying the inside of the boat and keeping both condensation and mould down to a fraction of what it was that first winter.

My duvet had become my arch nemesis. I hated it, and early on in our second year onboard, I began to search for an alternative. I had in mind some kind of eiderdown, preferably something that was mould resistant and would not absorb moisture. I hit upon the ideal product and I say that as we emerge from a long, wet winter, so I say it with confidence. If there is any community who spends a lot of time in miserable, wet conditions in all seasons, it is the fishing community. No matter the weather, our lakes, rivers and coastlines, are forever dotted with people fishing. So, it stands to reason that they would have the ideal bedding for cold, damp conditions. I duly had a look at the bedding they used and found and invested in a fantastic bedroll, complete with a fitted nylon skirt. Rated to minus 15 centigrade, it was costly, but the moment I slid into its fleece lining, I forgot the price and found myself grinning happily.

The crux of all our shivering and searching was that, by and large, we survived an icy first winter and learned a lot. By the second winter, we were so much better equipped and prepared thanks to all the newbie mistakes we had made. On reflection, there was probably only one 'solution' to the cold that we did not bother to attempt and that is the use of tealight candles. The idea is you burn the tiny candles under upturned terracotta flowerpots to generates heat and warm your boat. The flames will also generate carbon monoxide and burn up your oxygen. The idea is as dangerous as it is crazy.

Mad hatter plans and underpowered fan heaters aside, living on a boat through a freezing UK winter can be both comfortable and exhilarating. The canals and towpaths are largely deserted. The wildlife ventures closer, and there is something ethereal about a silent canal, iced with frost and padded by snow.

Summer on the water is payback for all the cold, muddy days of winter. Long days, stunning countryside scenes and cool refreshing drinks beside the barbecue. Our first summer was the warmest in forty years by all accounts, and we quickly discovered that a boat gets extremely warm when in full sun. Our neighbouring narrowboat owners sat gasping in the shade of the trees along the towpath, unwilling to climb aboard their boats, which were like tin ovens. People were recording temperatures in excess of fifty centigrade in their vessels. Temperatures this high were likely due to poor insulation. Nevertheless, discounting the extremes, even temperatures in the high thirties is no laughing matter.

Wyebourne has no fridge. What we used, instead, was a hardbody cooler box and a bag of ice bought from the local store. With careful packing, the ice would last two to three days. Still, we dared not keep meat for longer than a couple of days in the cooler and fortunately we eat and drink very little dairy. Being ultra-wary, we managed to survive the summer without any food poisoning or tummy upsets.

Just keeping our drinks cool and our salad greens fresh was not good enough though. We wanted to be able to pour an ice-cold drink anytime we liked. In the spring of 2019, going into our second summer on Wyebourne, I bought an electric cooler. This was the kind that runs off the 12V outlet (formerly known as a cigarette lighter) in a car. I had hoped that with the long summer days providing a steady flow of current through the solar panel, we'd be able to store perishables all week. Again, I was disappointed. The cooler draws too much power for very little benefit. Subsequently, I have discovered that a 12V fridge is a better option. The difference being that the fridge has a thermostat that causes the motor to kick in only when needed, thus saving on power.

I have also learned that using a cooler is not as simple as throwing in the meat, veggies, and drinks. There is definitely a right way to pack a cooler and, even without power, it can keep food fresh for days if used wisely.

We were moored up near the village of All Cannings for two weeks during our second summer. As I was strolling through the countryside, I noticed a grassy mound in the distance. Taking a closer look, I discovered it was a long barrow. Long barrows are Neolithic constructs that were used for funerary purposes, and there are numerous examples of these through the Vale of Pewsey. This one was far more recent than its five-thousand-year-old cousins and I discovered it had been built by a local just a couple of years earlier. Like its ancient predecessors, it was built to house the deceased - for a fee. The idea must have captured people's imagination because it was fully subscribed before its completion. The barrow is aligned to the Winter Solstice so that the rising sun illuminates the long interior passageway. There are footpaths that take walkers to the top of the barrow, and I followed one through the meadow grass and flowers to its highest point. In the late afternoon light, the countryside lay simmering in a golden haze.

Long summer evenings are ideal for relaxing barbecues. Better still, a barbecue beneath restful trees alongside a placid canal with birdsong all about us. Since there is nowhere to keep a traditional barbecue, I found a miniature fire bin for sale at a national hardware retail chain and it served as the barbecue, firepit and bin for storing kindling and briquettes. Multi-purposing items on a boat is a skill and this was a multipurpose trifecta.

Wyebourne had a serious problem when it came to early sunrises and hot sunny days. The curtains were made of flimsy cotton that you could practically see through. Privacy was scant and the sun would light up the cabin before 5am in the mornings. It was bad enough to prompt me to accompany my wife to a curtain retailer where I spent a painful couple of hours hunting for just the right fabric to make some real curtains from. In the end, we picked a neutral grey thermal material. Once a kind friend had sown these up, we not only had privacy and darkness, we also had an additional barrier against the cold.

If you take a walk along your nearest towpath, you'll be greeted by loads of narrowboats, cabin cruisers and barges, each displaying their owner's unique sense of style. Wanting to do something with our windows, I thought of capitalising on the long hours of sunlight. I've always enjoyed the light effects created by stained-glass, so I began to search for something similar to hang on our windows. I scrolled past numerous crystals and cheap looking stained-glass decorations until, by chance, I discovered a static film that could be cut to size and fitted to the inside of the windows. The film was patterned, and just like stained glass, it reflected colourful light. Over the course of an afternoon, I measured and fitted this film to the windows along our main cabin and in the galley. It was dead simple to work with and since it does not require an adhesive, it's ideal. The effect was exactly what I wanted, a patterned film that allowed light in, while offering us privacy and also creating beams of tranquil colours. On sunny mornings, we can now open the curtains and enjoy both the sun and privacy.

Moving from a house with reliable Wi-Fi to a boat where the only internet access is through mobile data, we were suddenly like fish out of water. It was embarrassing how little I knew about mobile data, streaming and dongles. Our mobile packages were wholly unfit for limited access Wi-Fi and we upped our mobile data package to ten gigabytes (GB) per month each. That was still not enough and we increased it to twenty GB per month each, the maximum our provider would allow us. This forced us to adapt and learn how to download movies and music whenever we were anywhere there was free Wi-Fi. If we went to a restaurant or even grocery shopping, the first thing we'd do was begin downloading our favourite movies, podcasts and music to enjoy once back on the boat. Likewise with images I needed to upload to my website.

Our provider must have felt our pain because without us asking, they upped our maximum usage to forty GB per month each in December 2019. What a great Christmas present that was.

CHAPTER 9
NEVER TOO OLD TO LEARN

Every day is a DIY day. Harvesting the sun. Craft skills and writer's block.

I have always enjoyed learning new skills and taking on new projects. In my opinion, this trait is a big positive when adapting to life as an off-grid boater. From the day I became a liveaboard boater, I have constantly been learning new skills, crafts and ways of doing things.

I mentioned in an earlier chapter that the boat came with a load of DIY material, primarily cans of paint, grease, and other products I had never had an occasion to use. Painting and decorating were old hat to me, but there were other skills I needed to learn or pay someone else to do.

The canopy that came with Wyebourne was serviceable, but the stitching was coming loose along the window panels and I really did not fancy dishing out a thousand pounds for a replacement canopy because some thread had perished. I had a look at what I needed online, watched a few videos and bought myself a hand bobbin and wax thread. Like all these things, there is a knack to it and the more you do it, the better at it you become. I began by sewing all the bits that were in danger of ripping further, especially around the door flaps. The damage contained, I then went into maintenance mode to keep the canopy together and try to limit the worst of the leaks. In case you are wondering, I have only stabbed myself once. If you saw the size of the needle needed to sew the canopy, you'd understand why once was all I needed to learn to keep my fingers clear of the pointy end.

My wife writes and illustrates children's books. Over long winter nights and quiet afternoons in summer, she has practised and perfected her character and background illustrations. This kind of creative pursuit is ideal for life onboard. It does not take up room and can be packed away or resumed in a few minutes.

Since moving onto Wyebourne, I have written and published four new titles including this book. Again, life onboard a boat along the quiet canals is perfect for focusing my creative energy on my work. After moving onto the boat, it was a real shift in routine, and I did worry for a while about if I could find the time to focus on writing. I was finalising the draft of the third title in the Sons of Iberia series at the time. With the extreme change of lifestyle, my mind was everywhere at once and I could barely sit still for five minutes, let alone string a sentence together. Everything was so new. The sound of the boat, the patterns of light reflected off the water onto the ceiling, the call of the rooks. Canoes would go past, rocking Wyebourne and I confess, I'd hop up to peer out the window. The chugging of an old Lister or Perkins engine would catch my attention and I'd pop onto the deck to watch a narrowboat pass and give my fellow boater a wave. The moorhen would give me a call, cyclists would stop on the towpath beside the boat, hikers would ramble by. I felt like one of those dashboard dolls with the bobbling head. It had to be done though. My readers need their fix. I need my fix. I get miserable when I don't write or write sporadically. I set up a folding desk on the stern deck beneath the canopy. Here, I could keep an eye on my surroundings while beavering away on my word count. I just needed to establish the rhythm and once I did that, I was back in the game. More than back in the game. I find the solitude of long stretches of the canal on weekdays is perfect for losing myself in the plots and scenery of the stories I write. I've discovered that it is not only us who are able to draw on beauty of the waterways for inspiration. There are loads of exceptional artists who live and work on their floating homes.

Keeping the boat warm and lights burning is crucial, and while the big inboard *Nanni* diesel engine can recharge the leisure batteries, I dislike running it for that purpose alone. Many boaters have no qualms with using their engines as generators, and they'll run them for a couple of hours every day. Etiquette requires that engines and generators only run between 8am and 8pm. I prefer to use my boat engine to get me from place to place and I find that the noise and vibration of the engine on a 25-foot fibreglass boat is intrusive.

To avoid the pollution and noise of using the engine as a generator, I bought a 100Watt solar panel and the kit necessary to wire it into the boat. I'd never done any electrical wiring before and I learned what I needed from watching videos online and reading up on internet forums. I built a wooden frame with decking boards to house the solar panel, fitted this to the roof of the main cabin and wired it into a bank of new leisure (deep-cycle) batteries. While we were away working during the day, the single 100Watt panel was fine for keeping the battery bank topped up so we could charge our devices in the evenings and on weekends. It was not up to the task once we were forced to work from home by the health emergency lockdown. Any two consecutive cloudy days would see the battery bank drop to 12.4V and it is unwise to allow the batteries to deplete further as this erodes their ability to take and hold a charge. Looking ahead, working from the boat over winter will prove even more challenging as the batteries will also need to power the diesel heater, which draws a lot of power.

I will need to add at least another 200Watts to the panels and a MPPT charge controller to maximise charging efficiency. It will also be an opportunity to modify the brackets holding the panels and I plan to build them from Galvanised Slotted Angle strips. This will look better than the decking board and I'll be able to adjust the angle of the solar panels to better catch the low winter sunshine.

The thing about living as an off-grid boater is to take advantage of power wherever you can. When we visit our son and daughter-in-law, for instance, at least one leisure battery, both power banks and all our COB headlamps come with us to recharge off the mains. The other opportunity to recharge batteries is when we drive anywhere. We have an inexpensive inverter which we plug into the car's 12V output plug (formerly known as the cigarette lighter). This allows us to charge our mobile phones, laptops and torches when we travel any distance.

While I am talking about recharging devices, I'll describe the primary lighting we use on Wyebourne. We have rarely ever used the boat's inbuilt lighting, which is ancient and meagre. Instead, we use solar powered outdoor lights. Each morning, I pop them onto the dashboard where they can catch the sun. At night before bed, I put one on a shelf in the main cabin and hang the other in the head. They are motion activated and light up the moment either of us step into the main cabin or go to the loo. I think this is crucial in case of emergencies and saves us from having to grope for a torch or light switch. We have a COB work lamp for evenings in the main cabin and this runs off rechargeable AA batteries which I recharge off the solar grid or the generator.

For navigation, we have the running lights which are powered by the starter battery as well as both a mast and a stern light. The mast light is especially useful for navigating tunnels. Bruce tunnel is the only tunnel we have passed through to date. It is 502 yards (459 meters) long and named after the landowner who did not want a canal cut through his estate but agreed to allow a tunnel beneath it. The commercial freight barges of the time relied on horses which would be harnessed to the barges and then tow the vessels as they plodded along the adjacent towpath. Since they couldn't pull the vessels through the tunnel, chains were attached to the roof of the tunnel and the boatmen would haul the barge along by pulling on these chains. I preferred our way, although Wyebourne would be a fraction of the weight of those old barges.

I was genuinely surprised at the cost of blankets, rugs and throws in retail outlets. When we went shopping for new curtain material, we priced throws and cushions and the prices stuck in my mind. This summer, I plan to make my own blanket and have begun to practice crochet. I can't remember what made me think of crochet, it might have been an impulse, but when I looked online at the feasibility of making a big woollen blanket, I was surprised and excited at the range of items that could be crocheted. Cushion covers, slippers, carpets, beanies. So far, I've learned to do a chain and a double stitch and as soon as the days are longer, I intend to make at least one big blanket. I also plan to experiment with different twines to make a hard-wearing rug for the stern deck.

My wife became interested in this craft at the same time and is already leaps and bounds ahead of me in skill. She has already crocheted a veritable wardrobe full of baby blankets, hoodies, and scarves for the family. Her latest project was a new winter scarf for me. She had found a yarn made from both sheep and alpaca wool and was keen to use this. She asked me to choose a colour or two and I did. A navy blue and a kind of mauve or lavender. Colours are not my strongpoint. However, when she began crocheting it, I was appalled that she kept referring to it as pink. I don't do pink. To settle the argument, I've posted a picture of online so that you can let us know what colour you think it is.

From crochet to unmentionables. We usually drop our laundry off at a franchise for washing and folding. A lot of boaters do have small washing machines onboard, but we simply do not have the space. In summer, I am happy to handwash clothes if the weather is favourable for drying the laundry afterwards. There are hand powered washing machines which use a fraction of the amount of detergent and water to wash a 5lb (2kg) load of laundry. The high revolution speed of the drum enables you to spin dry the clothes before hanging them out. Again, there is the space restriction onboard Wyebourne and even the smallest washer will take up precious room.

As a keen vegetable gardener, I have been growing our own vegetables on a privately owned allotment site for a few years. This all began when I built a small hydroponics setup in our garage. Throughout summer and autumn, our cupboards are full of leafy salads, tomatoes, chilies, and root vegetables. While I grow them readily enough and eat them with gusto, my wife is an expert at canning them. There is something very fulfilling about twisting the lid of a jar and hearing that loud pop that signals a well-preserved feast. Moving onto Wyebourne, I was excited to explore growing veggies onboard and looked forward eagerly to the new growing season. The moment the weather began to warm in April, I got busy. I laid out seed trays on the large dashboard under the windscreen and sowed tomatoes, chillies, and aubergines. Followed by squash, courgette, and beans. By late April, I had trays of seedlings ready for planting out on the allotment. I kept a handful of tomato and chilli plants back to grow on the boat in larger pots. The only other plant we had had was an aloe vera which had succumbed to the winter cold. My boat garden grew well enough, but the fruit took weeks longer to ripen than their tray-mates, which I planted out on the allotment. I suspect this might have been caused by the shadier conditions they grew in. Even though they were up on a pallet on the cabin roof, the leafy trees along the canal exclude the sunlight tomatoes need to ripen.

Another idea I have toyed with is to purchase a little

rowing boat and build a polytunnel on that. I have seen a tender used as a floating garden, so the idea is not entirely original.

The downside to growing plants on the boat is that there is already an overabundance of spiders onboard. Plant foliage will just attract even more of them and I don't care what anyone says, they always find their way into the bedroom.

Since moving onto Wyebourne, my nautical vocabulary has grown massively. That said, it being mid-April as I write this chapter; I have just discovered a new word. Fettling. What a great word it is, too. Spring is the time when boaters usually do their boat fettling and yes, between writing paragraphs and consuming coffee, I am fettling away like a happy little pirate. So next time you're down on the towpath and pass a boater scrubbing the decks or polishing the trim, you can wish them good fettling.

A big concern we had when we first moved onto Wyebourne was the issue of security. This was especially relevant when we both worked and were away from the boat, sometimes for the whole day. Researching life on the waterways of the UK, it became evident that in some places, boats and boaters are seen as soft targets for petty thieves and vandals. Boaters' groups on social media painted a grim picture. Boaters, especially liveaboard boaters, almost all rely on generators, wheelbarrows, and bicycles. It seemed that these were the items that most often grew legs and disappeared. Another common occurrence was returning to the boat to find that someone had syphoned all the diesel from the fuel tank. Another concern was the vandalism, which ranged from cutting mooring lines to actually breaking and entering. If your home, however small, has been broken into and your private possessions tipped into heaps on the floor, you'll be familiar with the emotions experienced by the victims. So often, the vandals smash and slash furniture and fittings, and even defecate on objects. The worst was the wanton destruction of boats by arsonists who would set fire to them.

With these horror stories in mind, it was awfully hard to moor Wyebourne and drive away knowing we'd be gone for eight or more hours. Seeing Wyebourne sunk, burned or damaged by storm would be excruciating enough. Knowing that someone did the damage for kicks or to steal something would be ten times worse.

Determined not to be easy targets, we researched the market for deterrents and alarms. Our first line of defence are stickers cautioning that Wyebourne is alarmed. The second is the door keypad, which will sound if someone tries to force the door. It is uncomfortably loud, as I discovered when I was too slow entering the pin code. The third is the real time security camera footage sent to my mobile phone, which allows me to witness any unauthorised entry onto the boat.

As great as these all are, the best defence is the numerous eyes and ears of the boating community. It is not unlike a village where everyone knows your comings and goings and if they see a stranger kicking about on a boat; they are ready and willing to get involved.

A recent example of how this canal-telegraph works involved a stolen boat, a dog, and dozens of boaters up and down the Kennet and Avon. Contrary to lockdown advice, a narrowboat cruised past us one lunchtime. Passing beneath a bridge and through the nearby lock, he then moored up in the stretch of water above us. A short while later, he took exception to a lady who had stopped on the bridge to take a photo of the canal as people frequently do. It became very apparent from his barrage of yelling and cursing that he was not in a good place. A little while later, he began calling for the little dog that he had with him, and it was with some relief that we heard him start up his boat and leave. The following morning, liveaboards a few miles west of us began reporting that the same boater had arrived at the lock where they were moored. That lock was out of commission and had been for weeks, but despite the warning signs, barriers and advice from the live aboard boaters, he tried to force his way through. In doing so, he only succeeded in flooding the lower stretch of water and draining the stretch he and the rest of the boaters were in, leaving everyone's boats canted on a bed of gravel and mud. The fuss terrified his little dog, which sought a quiet place on a kindly boater's bed. The abusive language and threat of damage forced someone to call the police, who arrived to calm down frayed tempers and send the rogue boater packing back the way he had come with his dog. By now, everyone on the canal knew of the drama and reports of his anti-social behaviour elsewhere surfaced. Many boaters were as concerned about the dog's welfare as they were about the bloke's. Very soon, somebody mentioned that a boat had been stolen near Reading and descriptions were circulated. Sure enough, it was the boat the rogue boater was captaining. To add to the drama, he was not causing chaos by not properly closing the locks, flooding and draining stretches as he went. He passed us in the dark, heading the opposite way, and as he went, boaters reported his location and minded the locks to prevent damage. By lunchtime, the police stepped in to recover the stolen boat while the bloke was detained and given the care he needed. His little dog was taken care of and re-homed.

There is very little that happens on the canal that does not quickly become common knowledge and boaters usually the first to come to each other's aid and to protect one another's property as well as the canal infrastructure and wildlife.

CHAPTER 10
FROM DROUGHT TO FLOOD

Rivers, storms, floods, droughts, and gales

At 3am one winter morning, I was woken by the sound of swirling splashes beneath the boat. Afraid that Wyebourne was taking on water, I raced to the stern deck with a torch to peer over the side. It was eerily quiet with a thick mist floating over the canal and yet the water along the side of the boat was unsettled, as though the boat was trembling. Then the worst thing I could imagine happened; bubbles started streaming up from beneath the boat. Wyebourne had surely sprung a leak below the waterline and was sinking. A heartbeat before I could react, a face followed the bubbles to emerge from the water, just inches from mine. Large, dark eyes fixed on the beam of torchlight before its face turned to meet my stare. Shocked, we both screamed and recoiled in fright. And that's how I met my first wild otter.

As mentioned in earlier chapters, the year we bought and moved onto Wyebourne saw the longest and most severe drought the UK has experienced in decades. For us, this meant not just weeks of sunny weather, but almost three months of blue skies and never a drop of rain. We could not have asked for a more comfortable initiation into life on a boat. In a way, it also gave us a false sense of security because summers do not last forever, and winter is just a season away.

One of my biggest concerns when I took Wyebourne out for a test run on the Thames prior to offering, was the height of the river. If you do not live on a flood plain, or close to a river, it's easy to underestimate just how capricious flowing water can be. The current can go from a sluggish drift to a raging torrent in an hour. Yesterday's rainfall in the upper catchment area might mean that tomorrow a wide swath of land miles downstream is flooded.

As a boater, the importance of understanding the river and the flow of water cannot be overstated enough. Before we came down the Thames, I read that boats should be moored facing into the current. With this advice in mind, after identifying a favourable place to moor each evening, I'd turn back upriver so that Wyebourne's bow pointed upstream. In this way, instead of the current dangerously dragging on the square stern of the boat, it is parted smoothly by the shape of the hull. Tying the mooring lines becomes so much easier as you are not constantly straining on the rope as you tie off. This was emphasized at Fobney Lock when we met a couple on a narrowboat from up north. They had come off the Grand Union Canal in Oxford and cruised down the Thames behind us. I noticed the gentleman favouring his left hand and he sheepishly explained that the previous evening; they had moored up facing downstream. While tying up, the current caught the boat, trapping his hand between the iron bollard and the taut mooring line. If you consider the enormous weight of a steel narrowboat, he was lucky to free his hand and only suffer bruising.

One of the tips the hire boat company employee gave us that stuck in my mind was to look out for water flowing into the canal or river. What happens is that as you pass this inflow, it strikes your vessel from the side and if you are not prepared, can wash you up against the opposite bank. On the last day of our hire boat trip, the heavens opened, and it bucketed down for all it was worth. I gamely stood alone at the helm as the tempest raged about me. Okay, perhaps not quite a tempest, but I was soaked right through to my unmentionables. As we chugged into the outskirts of Devizes, I noticed a strong stream of water gushing from a storm drain and surging across the width of the canal. I eased the bow towards the incoming stream and throttled up the engine a notch. Sure enough, as soon as the narrowboat met the surge, it lurched and was driven back into the centre of the canal. If I had not taken the precaution I did, the current could have washed the vessel into shallow water or onto a mudbank. Apart from the validation of this navigational tip, I also realised with growing clarity, how connected we would be to the elements as liveaboard boaters. Bright, sunny days will always be great, but to be comfortable, we'd need to embrace all kinds of weather and stop regarding rainy days or freezing nights as miserable. A more open mindset to the weather would go a long way to keeping our spirits up throughout the year.

Coming up the Kennet and Avon Canal a year later in our cabin boat, we had none of these surges and currents to worry about. One place that is notorious among boaters is Midgham Lock at Woolhampton. Here, the Kennet River sweeps in from the left just as they navigate through the swing bridge located there. If the river is running high, they need all the power they can muster to stay on course for the lock gates or risk either ricocheting off brickwork or being grounded in the opposite shallows. When we passed through, the river was barely flowing and navigating through to the lock was a doddle.

The change in weather was inevitable at some point, and it occurred with a terrifying storm. It was September, and we had been loving life on Wyebourne for four months. Moving regularly west along the Kennet and Avon Canal, we were moored just west of Hamstead Lock. It was a stunning location and on the actual river rather than on one of the stretches of man-made canal. As there were already other boats there, I was forced to moor beneath a tree. After tying up, I had a good look at the tree, which looked sturdy with no dead limbs or heavy vine growth. Neither was it leaning over the canal. As it happened, the weather remained settled until the following Thursday evening. On that night, the first named storm of the season struck with a vengeance. In no time, I was cursing that tree and myself for mooring under it. Storm Ali, as it was christened by the Met Office, began with a stiff breeze in the early evening, which had the canopy snapping and billowing. At 9pm that night, as I was doing a final check of the mooring pins, I eyed the swaying branches above the boat with trepidation and briefly considered moving Wyebourne. Boats had moved on since we had arrived at the spot, so there was space further along where we could moor, but I felt moving in the conditions would be more dangerous than staying in place. To say we never slept a wink may be an exaggeration, but not by much. It seemed the moment my head touched the pillow; the rain began to belt down and the strong breeze turned into a frenzied gale. I couldn't decide which disaster would strike us first. There were so many to choose from! The canopy was booming like a bass drum at a heavy metal concert. The boat was lurching and thumping the mooring below the waterline. The river level was rising and the tree above us was raining branches down on the cabin roof with intent. If I looked anything like my wife, I was pale, twitching, and my eyes were as big as saucers. Plus, I was cursing. I especially swore when I heard the nasty pop of a tree breaking in half in the nearby woodland.

As Wyebourne was battered against the bank, each thump seemed to vibrate through my feet. Gritting my teeth, I went out in the lashing rain and howling wind to try to lodge a larger fender between the mooring and her hull. That proved impossible though, because the fender just floated over the side of the mooring thanks to the raised water level. As I was clambering into and out of the canopy door, I noticed a darker shadow on the water. Rubbing rain out of my eyes, I realised it was a duck who had wisely decided to ride the storm out in the lee of the boat. The moment I saw that duck, I noticed there was a whole flock of fellow ducks bobbing there in the dark, thankful for the meagre shelter Wyebourne offered.

Daylight came at last, and while the wind was still strong, it was much tamer. The cabin roof was littered with a carpet of leaves and twigs. From the sounds they had made landing on the roof, I thought I'd find a woodpile of branches as thick as my thigh. The boat was fine. We were exhausted, but thankful that nothing serious had happened. Without discussion, we pulled up the mooring pins and moved the boat to a spot with no overhanging branches. As it turned out, the worst of the storm was felt across Ireland, Wales, and Northern England and there were sadly two fatalities caused by the high gales.

In the two years we have lived aboard Wyebourne, we have experienced a lot of bad weather and frightening storms, but it's true what they say. You never forget your first.

I've never been sold on snow and less so when living on Wyebourne. In January 2019, it became bitterly cold and the canal froze over. Thankfully, I had the diesel heater up and running by then and could stave off frostbite and hypothermia. The frosty mornings with the sun low on the horizon were stunning. The one thing that looked grim was the canal water. It looked like soapy dishwater that had frozen. The forecast for the last weekend of January was snow, lots of it. We decided a break from the relentless weather was a good idea and booked a hotel room for the weekend. Long hot showers, all the power the national grid could throw at us, and takeaway dinners sounded perfect. Waking up on Friday morning, I knew immediately that it had snowed. That particular muffled silence indicative of deep snow penetrated our cabin and found me huddled beneath my duvet, clutching a hot water bottle that had long since cooled. Looking out the windows was a waste of time since they were iced up. I shivered my way up onto the stern deck and forced the zipper on the frozen canopy. Snow covered the towpath, the boat, and everything I shone my torch at. We were moored outside a tiny village, surrounded by steep hills. Every road out was uphill. I warned my wife that the trip would be hairy as I prepared to put the car and my driving to the test. On the way up the towpath, we passed a fellow boater walking his German Shepard. He looked at us pityingly, shook his head and gave us zero chance of getting out of the valley. What he didn't know was how incentivised I was by the prospect of a weekend in a hotel room. The snow was half a foot deep on the road. As we all know, in the UK anything deeper than three inches is enough to bring traffic to a skidding halt. Swallowing hard, I cleared the car of snow, packed our luggage for our short hotel stay, and started up the engine. I edged the car onto the road, my knuckles white. At once, the back of the car threatened to fishtail and I changed up a gear. Up the hill I drove, keeping the car at a steady speed in as high a gear as possible. I was determined to reach that hotel. There were a few tense moments as I took some tight corners, but it went better than expected and ten minutes later, we reached the gritted main road. Traffic was almost non-existent that morning as the country woke to a blanket of snow and people declared it a snow-day. We duly checked into the hotel to enjoy hot water and the much fantasised-about surplus of electricity.

2019 started off cold and then, crazily, we had a weird warm spell in February. When I say warm, I mean the daytime temperature rose to a balmy eighteen degrees Celsius. I loved it, but I'm wary of out of the ordinary weather. The following day the temperatures dropped to their usual low single digits.

I have always marvelled at the change of seasons and

none is more dramatic than the winter to spring metamorphosis. This change feels so much more remarkable when living on a boat and being so close to nature. The first change is the lengthening of the daylight hours. For us who rely so heavily on solar power for our heating and appliances, this is a big change. By the middle of February, I can see a big increase in the sunlight harvested and the green charge controller lights look so much brighter.

As the sun rises higher and the days lengthen, the warming water causes a bloom of algae which coats everything beneath the waterline in billowy olive-green growth. This carpet of algae dies off from late March. As it dies and rots, it breaks up into slimy looking clumps that float to the surface. It is not unusual to see the downwind surface of the canal covered by the dead vegetation. The warming water also sees gas bubbling up from the depths of the canal as methane is released. Along the waterside, swans chase their offspring from the season before, the moorhens' combs become a vivid red and the blackbird leads the dawn chorus. In the fields beyond the canal, hares begin their ritual boxing and deer stand thawing in patches of early morning sunlight. Closer to the boat, spiders shake out their webs while bumble bees cruise along the banks seeking nests. In April, hornets wake with a furious hunger and begin hunting. If you sit still and watch them, they are fascinating. They cruise from one likely spot to the next, seeking their favourite prey, spiders. I've watched one the size of my thumb, systematically scan the pointing between bricks on a lock, looking for spiders the blue tits might have missed. Sounding like a helicopter gunship, it turned its attention to me and briefly paused at each of my nostrils before whipping off into the distance. Apparently, my nostrils qualify as spider dens. If I'm honest, I am not sure how I feel about that.

Then came the Easter bank holiday. It turned out to be a sunny, warm Easter weekend. We were moored near Pewsey and excited to have front row seats for the Devizes to Westminster canoe race. The conditions proved a real struggle for the contestants with the warm weather and an easterly wind. Easter passed and the clouds came back and stayed right through summer, proving my unease at the erratic weather well-founded.

The clouds cleared for July, but after that it was more of the same and from September on the weather became very blustery. All through autumn, winter and into spring of the following year, the wind never seemed to let up. By now, I knew to steer clear of mooring under trees! This didn't lessen the noise though as gales lashed the boat, making the canopy snap and crack. On the first sunny day in weeks, I managed to treat the Oxford Cloth fabric with a coat of paint-on water-repellent. The coating was no sooner dry when the rain began to fall again. The following morning, I was gratified to see perfect beads of water decorating the outside of the canopy, which proved it was once again waterproof. I was not finished sewing the various loose panels on the canopy either. With my time stretched between my day job and revising the final edits of the fourth book in the Sons of Iberia series by night, I took a shortcut. I bought a special adhesive tape. There is an old DIY joke that says the only two essentials any DIY'er really needs are duct tape and WD40. In this case, the tape was incredibly expensive, but by all accounts, extremely durable. If there is one word I like when making a purchase, it is the word durable.

Why this need to ensure the canopy was waterproof? It covers the stern deck of the boat which is about a third of our entire living space. I don't spend much time there in winter, but it's where we store our footwear, and other items that need to be kept dry. Also, any water ingress will pool in the bilge below the deck and ice up.

The tape duly arrived, and I was underwhelmed by its appearance. I had only purchased 3 meters and it looked like a folded note tucked into a cardboard envelope. Carefully following instructions, unusual for me, I cut and applied it ever so carefully, sealing all tears around the plastic windows. Almost a year later, much of the tape is still holding and should last until the new canopy arrives in time for the coming winter.

CHAPTER 11
STAYING HEALTHY

The sunniest summer ever. Long walks and exercise. Bugs that lurk. A good torch and boots. Wheelbarrows save backs.

The one constant along the Kennet and Avon Canal from March to November is the presence of nettles along the towpath. I first discovered how prevalent they were on the canal when we hired a narrowboat in 2017. Since moving onto Wyebourne, it is rare that a week goes by without me wincing at least once or twice as I brush against their stings. While repinning Wyebourne on a soft bank at Spooky Woods near Pewsey, I failed to notice a nettle among the other growth. As I bent to hammer the pin in, it stung me in the face from my ear to my mouth. That was a fun moment, although oddly not as painful as when I hopped off Wyebourne's stern and stepped on young nettle plants just emerging from the grass. The stings caught both the sole and top of my bare foot. The following morning my foot still throbbed sullenly. The lesson is don't tread on nettles, but more importantly, wear footwear on the towpath.

The summer of 2018 was the warmest and driest in 40

years, with weeks of blue skies and sunshine. Us humans are not the only creatures that enjoy warm weather, though. Uncooked meat will spoil in hours when it is warm and the temperatures in the galley often reach the early thirties, even when I am onboard with the door and windows open. When the boat is locked, it can exceed over forty degrees Celsius inside if the sun is shining. In these conditions, I have to be especially mindful of food poisoning through E. coli, salmonella, and even Listeria.

We do not have a fridge onboard Wyebourne and in such warm conditions, it's impossible to keep uncooked meat for longer than a few hours. What we did do that worked very well was to buy a bag of supermarket ice and keep this in a cool box. This allowed us to keep meat, dairy and fresh greens at 4 degrees Celsius for up to three days. Through 2018 and 2019, I noticed a surge of Listeria cases in the UK which was alarming and was a big incentive to cook our own meals. Listeria is a bacterium which causes listeriosis, an infection with some nasty symptoms and even fatal in combination with underlying health conditions. It is usually spread in unpasteurised milk, or dairy products made from unpasteurised milk, and in chilled ready-to-eat foods.

We have always found that hot weather like we had that summer reduces our appetites and is a great opportunity to reduce meat consumption and eat more salads. I grow a lot of our own produce, but when purchasing from supermarkets, we take special care to rinse vegetables thoroughly, especially leafy greens which are eaten uncooked. This is good practice in any circumstance, but especially when living off-grid as being ill in such a confined space as our boat can be very unpleasant.

Water was another source of possible contamination that we had to be alert to. Wyebourne has a two-hundred litre water tank which is plumbed to the sink and shower. We treat this water with purifying tablets and use it only for washing and rinsing. Even that can be a risk if the water is not cycled through the system often and left to stand for a week or more. If that happens, I find it safest to drain and flush the tank before refilling with fresh water.

Living on a boat and cruising along the Kennet and Avon Canal gives us access to endless miles of paths to explore. Right from the day I decided to become a liveaboard boater, I mentally shifted from existing in a brick cube to embracing all of my new environment. Unlike in town, where walking around the houses just felt odd, in the countryside I am comfortable hopping off the boat for a twenty minute or twenty-mile walk, whatever suits my mood and time. It's the perfect way to clear my head after sitting and writing scenes and chapters. Brisk walks obviously also have the added benefit of improving fitness and health. When we began living as Continuous Cruisers on the Kennet and Avon Canal, I'd walk the towpath, scouting out new places to moor, interesting venues along the canal, or just to soak up the scenery. Before long, I was wandering off along bridal paths and hiking routes, becoming familiar with the wider countryside.

Aside from the exercise, watching the wildlife is a great pleasure while walking. One of the scenes I witnessed while hiking through Spooky Woods outside Pewsey still has me chuckling whenever I think of it. It was a summery day and early in the morning. I was just returning from the wharf where I had deposited our refuse in the CRT bins. Ahead of me, the leafy boughs stretched across the still water of the canal. As I walked, I periodically tapped my walking stick to alert any herons or moor hens ahead of me. Despite doing this, I still startled a squirrel, for there was a sudden flurry of leaves in a branch way up over the canal, followed by a high-pitched chittering. Then, with a desperate, squirrelly scream, the little rodent lost its grip and fell out of the tree to land with an impressive belly flop in the centre of the canal.

I had once been standing beneath a tree looking up at a squirrel that had fallen a few feet towards my face before catching itself. At the time, I thought that was a one off.

Generally, watching squirrels nimbly bounce around in the tallest trees, I would never have guessed that they could slip and fall. After seeing this unfortunate creature also take a dive into the canal, I guess it happens more often than I thought. It must have plunged twelve foot or more through the air, and despite the belly flop, it went a good way below the surface. I arrived adjacent to where it had submerged to peer with concern into the ripples. A minute later it erupted from beneath the water and began paddling furiously to the bank. Directly towards where I stood. One look into its eyes was enough to convince me to scramble out of its way. I think it blamed me for its misfortune and it looked ready to take a bite out of my ankle.

They say you're never further than a few feet from a rat. This is easy to forget when living in a brick and mortar house in town. They are not so easy to forget when you open the lid of a skip and they come boiling out. I quite respect rats. Intelligent, adaptable, and resilient. They unfortunately also carry disease and are always scavenging for easy pickings. This is one reason I keep the decks clean and try to never leave bagged refuse overnight. They have an extremely acute sense of smell and have been trained to detect landmines buried for years in old conflict zones. Old salami wrappers and stale peanut butter sandwiches are like a clarion call to them. They will come. Shimmying up the mooring lines and crawling under the canopy. There is something genuinely creepy about the very distinct scrabble of a rat's claws along the gunwales. Mice are equally ambitious little pirates, and just recently we were boarded and raided by one. The prize? My newly sown butternut and cucumber seeds. I bring the trays off the cabin roof and onto the stern deck in the evenings. Taking them out one morning, I noticed seed husks on the surface of each container. I suspected it was a mouse at once. The little blighter had gone from container to container to dig out each seed for the kernel inside. I was especially insulted as I had used all my butternut seeds and had no more. I had hoped to be able to feed my grandson some delicious organic butternut that autumn. Getting more seed would be a challenge due to the lockdown in place to combat Covid-19. Fortunately, there was half a butternut in the galley and I was able to scoop out the seeds from that. I placed them on a kitchen towel to dry beneath the windscreen and stupidly neglected to pack them away after dark. Sure enough, the mouse had a feast that night, leaving behind a mound of empty husks. Declaring war, I constructed a simple trap consisting of a broom handle over a bucket. Baited with peanut butter, the idea is the rodent ventures onto the pole and when it tries to reach the bait, the pole rolls and deposits the thief in the bucket. It has worked on my allotment, but so far these country mice seem nimbler than their city cousins.

Lugging stuff between the car and the boat has become second nature. Loads of boaters have wheelbarrows for this purpose, but I went with a sack trolley because it could fold flat. I learned the hard way to make use of the tools at our disposal one Easter weekend. I had bought a new leisure battery to install on the boat. Parking as near as possible to Wyebourne, I still needed to lug the twenty-five kilogram battery a good three hundred yards. Not wanting to endure the clattering of the trolley along the uneven towpath, I opted to carry the battery slung in a kitbag around my neck. That twenty-five kilograms got heavy fast, but I managed to heave it onboard, huffing and puffing. The following day, I rolled out of bed and after breakfast went and sat on the front of the boat for half an hour to enjoy the sun. That was when my back decided to punish me for my stupidity and began to spasm. The rest of that bank holiday weekend was spent trying to find a comfortable position to sit, stand and sleep in. Lesson well learned!

On the subject of sleep, the quality of my sleep onboard Wyebourne is usually top notch. The gentle harmony of muted splashing, whispering leaves and the almost imperceptible movement of the boat combine to give a natural ASMR experience. ASMR stands for autonomous sensory meridian response and is a pleasant sensation that causes relaxation. There are times when sleep is harder to achieve, such as when a howling gale beats at the canopy like a drum. Occasionally, the fenders will rub the wrong way between the lush vegetation beside the canal and the boat's hull. At one place, the strangest tapping and sucking sound occurred all night right beside my head. The urge to go outside and adjust the fenders and mooring lines was tempered by the thought of the stinging nettles that grew in that foliage. Right along with the desire to avoid being stung on my bare, cold feet, was the repulsion of standing on a fat slug. So instead, I covered my head with a pillow and concentrated on my breathing while vowing to sort it in the morning. Naturally, this annoying sound faded away with daylight, making my adjustments to the fenders a hit and miss effort, and it was impossible to see what had caused the odd sound. What I've taken to doing in the last year is using Wyebourne's mud anchor. Once moored up, I unleash the anchor, taking great delight in lobbing it into the canal with a weighty splash. With a happy chuckle, I then tauten the anchor rope, which drags Wyebourne's hull away from the vegetation that causes most of the noise. Dropping the anchor is also a simple way to prevent Wyebourne from being washed into the shallows by large boats as they pass.

The long, wet winter of 2019 seemed to start in September. It did not snow, nor did the canal freeze over, but the weather remained grey and it rained continuously. December, January and February saw an average of 469.7mm of rainfall, making it the fifth wettest winter on record according to the Met Office.

By March, I needed sunshine. I wanted to be able to walk somewhere, anywhere, without sliding in mud. When the sun did at last make an appearance in March 2020, it was to find the whole world, including the UK, in a very bad way.

In January, I picked up on reports from China concerning an infection that was causing severe pneumonia in people. Within days, the tone of the posts changed as Chinese medics treating patients also became ill with the virus. Creating a list of reliable sources of information on the epidemic, I watched with concern as the Chinese response became more and more surreal. In January, with a sense of foreboding, I bought three little bottles of hand sanitizer and raised the subject with my colleagues at work. By early February, the impact of the virus was still a world away in China with just a handful of known cases in other countries. Governments in Europe and elsewhere did not seem in the least bit concerned, and it was all business as usual. In the meantime, unknown to everyone, the virus was spreading undetected in Northern Italy.

We never keep more than a week's worth of food on the boat, preferring fresh ingredients to canned food. On 24 February, I decided I needed to stock a reserve of canned goods and dry provisions in case the situation in England became dire. On top of this emergency larder, which I stashed away on the boat, I bought extra food and essentials every time I shopped. In the middle of March, the rest of the country caught on and *panic-buying* ensued. I italicised panic-buying because I don't think the run on food and provisions was driven by panic so much as people just wanting to be prepared. In any event, that is just my opinion, and the media led the charge in demonising people for stockpiling. Events happened quickly after that, and by March, it was clear that Europe and the world would be in for a ghastly summer.

Like the government, supermarkets and their supply chains were caught napping and within a couple of days, retail outlet shelves were empty. Shops were rarely fully stocked after the middle of March and I again bought only fresh food, confident we had a decent supply of canned and dry provisions to see us through any potential supply disruption. There really is not a lot of spare space on a 25-foot boat, and our food supply was probably enough to feed us for six to eight weeks at a push.

We had spent winter moored in the village of Great Bedwyn in Wiltshire, and as soon as I had recovered from a minor surgery, began to cruise west, intending to reach the *long pound* by April. This meant we were moored west of the village when the government in England finally took active steps to contain the spread of the virus.

On Tuesday 17 March, the UK government advised people to work from home where possible, to practice social distancing, and to only leave their homes where essential. That weekend, the skies cleared and the weather turned mild for the first time in months. Sun-starved people flocked to parks, beaches, and the countryside. Despite being outside the nearest village and miles from any large urban centre, the towpath came alive with walkers. By walkers, I don't mean the zombie kind. I mean people looking for peace and harmony away from the hysteria of the media. People who wanted to stretch their legs and enjoy the sun and fresh air. An ugly mood swept across the country as people took it upon themselves to decipher the government's rather mixed messages. We were horrified at the vigilante-like attitudes of people who began to hound *vanlifers* in the countryside and even in towns. The influx of people to towpaths also set off a minority of boaters who wanted the towpaths closed to the public. Emotions began to run high with some nasty confrontations reported.

I was fortunate in that I could work remotely, provided I could receive a decent Wi-Fi signal. In two years, I had only ever relied on my mobile phone data to access the internet while onboard. This would not be sufficient for work purposes and so I purchased a dongle with unlimited data and improved Wi-Fi reception.

Working from the boat placed new strains on our resources as we do not have access to the national grid through shore power. The single 100W solar panel I had installed the year before could not generate enough power to keep our laptops and mobile phones charged and, even though I stopped using the diesel heater to conserve electricity, the leisure batteries quickly began to drain. I have always been reluctant to run the inboard *Nanni* diesel engine for hours on end to charge the bank of leisure batteries. Now, fearing the situation would deteriorate even further; I opted to purchase a power generator. Bearing in mind my previous experience with a generator, I hesitantly ordered a small 1000W portable generator. It offered enough power to recharge the leisure batteries when needed, as well as run the laptops. It is what is described as a briefcase generator due to its compact size and minimal weight. I was fortunate that I ordered it when I did because it arrived on the day the country was locked down.

On the evening of Monday, 23 March, the prime minister strengthened the government's message and declared a lockdown across the entire country. The public would only be permitted to leave their homes to undertake key jobs, for essential shopping or to exercise. The Canal and River Trust advised Continuous Cruisers that the lockdown meant we should not move our boats except for essentials such as pumping out waste tanks and refilling water.

How did I feel about working from onboard Wyebourne? Previous to the outbreak of Covid-19, I had been reluctant to consider it as I preferred a boundary between what I did for a living and my private life. On the positive side, I would not have to commute 90-minutes a day to and from work, which would result in a nice saving in fuel and motoring costs. The downside was that my home would become my office, which may not sound like a big deal, but it is for me. My life on the boat is spontaneous and I rarely sit still for longer than an hour. Bringing my job into my home environment would require me to be more disciplined and adhere to timekeeping not of my choosing. This may sound trivial, but I believe that details like these contribute to a person's overall sense of well-being. Perhaps the prevailing poor mental health is caused by the loss or deprivation of this type of freedom?

The exercise was probably a good final test on the feasibility of working for a living from a boat. Now that I could not commute to work, for the most dystopian reason I could have imagined, I had turned Wyebourne into our office, complete with sturdy folding desks, good seating to maintain posture, internet access, and electricity to power our devices. We were unbelievably fortunate too. Many of our fellow boaters are self-employed in trades such as carpentry and engineering. Their work dried up overnight. The boaters that could still work were employed in office roles, NHS and care work, and retail and delivery. The big question was answered, though. I could work onboard Wyebourne and it proved to be comfortable as well as a big saving on commuting time and cost.

Across the UK, people were stepping up to help. Common symptoms of the virus were a persistent dry cough and fever. Those with suppressed immune systems were most at risk and mortality rates were highest among people over sixty. Community groups were formed to do essential shopping for the vulnerable or those self-isolating because they showed symptoms. Julian House, a charity which offers aid to the homeless and also supports traveller and liveaboard communities, sent out a call for community helpers to coordinate with liveaboard boaters during the crisis. Since I had none of the symptoms and was not particularly at risk, I was glad to volunteer. It was an opportunity to support fellow boaters who were appreciative of the safety net offered to them by the charity. The role was mostly hiking along the canal to check if any of the more vulnerable boaters needed prescriptions or shopping collected. In some instances, boaters whose livelihoods had vanished overnight due to the lockdown needed food parcels. There was also a fantastic pay-it-forward initiative for coal, fuel and gas set up with the local fuel boats. Boaters who could afford to, bought an extra one of anything they were buying; gas, coal etc, and the fuel boat owners would then have a stock of paid-for essentials they could give to any boaters struggling financially.

My lasting memory of the volunteer work during the lockdown is of the smiles and nods of liveaboards. While appreciative of the charity's help, for the most part they were already looking out for one another, doing each other's shopping, sharing coal, or just being a nearby light in the dark. It was humbling to realise that I had become a part of such a special community.

CHAPTER 12
LONG TERM PLANS AND BON VOYAGE

Revamping Wyebourne. Buying a larger boat. Cruising the waterways of Europe. Bon voyage.

As I write this chapter after two years of living on our amazing Wyebourne, I already look forward to future experiences and challenges. There is so much more to learn about boating and there is a wide world beyond our horizons, ripe for exploration. The great danger is that I have already become too settled onboard Wyebourne and before I know it, five years will have passed. To avoid that from happening, I have some dreams I like to think of as long term plans.

As comfortable as Wyebourne has been, with the rudimentary plumbing and electrics, it is one step up from camping and possibly not as comfortable as many glamping experiences. I need to improve the shower and modernize the battery bank and wiring through the boat. The light fittings are the original fittings from the sixties and I would like to strip them out and upgrade to cob lighting throughout. The trick is knowing how much to upgrade before we trade up for a more spacious vessel.

Ideally, I would like a 32-foot GRP with an aft cabin and a large centre cockpit enclosed with a hardtop. This would give us that additional space to have our son and his young family over, as well as give us more room to work comfortably on new projects.

In time, I would like to explore further afield. Since we both work in Wiltshire, we have not yet cruised the hundreds of miles of waterways north of the Thames and we would love to be able to do that. Europe, too, has an extensive canal and river system that stretches from the far North all the way down to the Mediterranean Sea.

How amazing would it be to spend the summer months in the north and then follow the birds south to the coast ahead of winter? This was one of the thoughts that originally persuaded me to look more closely into living on a boat. Watching videos posted by boaters of themselves enjoying sunny summer days cruising canals such as the *Canal du Midi*, in France or the *Mittelland Canal* in Germany, I can easily picture cruising among them.

Whatever comes next, I am sure it will be both challenging and exciting, and I am already looking forward to it.

That is the end of this leg of our tale and I hope you have enjoyed reading about our adventure. If you are thinking about moving onto a boat, I hope our experience has not put you off! Just the opposite. If you think this could be the life for you, go for it. Life is all about experiences and if we could make the change and survive, than I'm sure almost anybody can.

I will keep you updated on life on a yoghurt pot via my website where I will happily answer questions about life on a boat on an English canal.

Bon Voyage!

Glenn

CHAPTER 13
THE KENNET AND AVON CANAL

Its history. Some facts and figures. Wildlife.

This 87-mile-long waterway links Reading on the Thames with the Bristol Channel, passing through the visually stunning landscape of Wiltshire and the Cotswolds. The Kennet & Avon Canal includes three linked waterways, the Kennet River, the Avon River and the Kennet & Avon Canal.

The idea for the link between the Rivers Kennet and Avon was conceived in Elizabethan times. After the English Civil War, members of the aristocracy, farmers and traders feared water transport would reduce the fees they earned from turnpike roads, or that cheaper produce from Wales would undercut locally produced food. Some concerns never change!

In 1724 boats could travel up the River Kennet from Reading to Newbury, and from Bristol to the city of Bath on the River Avon by 1727. Linking these two rivers was the stuff of dreams and would mean a navigable system that reached from Bristol all the way to London.

The Kennet and Avon Canal included the Dundas and Avoncliff aqueducts, the Bruce Tunnel beneath Savernake

Forest, the pumping stations at Claverton and Crofton, and finally, the iconic Caen Hill Locks at Devizes. Three centuries of dreaming became reality in 1810 after sixteen years of work, with the construction of the canal and locks in Devizes to link the two river courses.

Among the two hundred working boats on the canal were seventy sixty-ton barges, hauling coal and quarried aggregate. At that time, the journey from Bath to Newbury took three and a half days. At the height of its commercial use, an average of 360,000 tons of freight was hauled by barge on the canal.

Passengers were able to get berths on Fly Boats which would take them between Bath and London in a non-stop four-day journey.

The coming of the Great Western Railway (GWR) thirty years later, put an end to the canal as a commercial route. As the working barges disappeared, pleasure boats began to ply those stretches of the canal still navigable from the 1920s.

During the dark days of the Second World War, following the British evacuation from Dunkirk, the Kennet and Avon Canal was designated GHQ Stop Line Blue. This was one of the lines of resistance strengthened to defend against an expected German invasion. Concrete pillboxes were built on the northern slopes and banks of the canal, guarding rail and road bridges the enemy would need to use to cross the canal. Many of these pillboxes still exist and are often easily visible, hunkering down in the middle of random fields or forests.

The canal was reopened in 1990 after years of hard work by the volunteers of The Kennet and Avon Canal Trust, local people, boaters, and waterway enthusiasts. On 8 August 1990, Queen Elizabeth II formally reopened the canal and was able to travel on the Trust's boat, The Rose of Hungerford, through locks 44 and 43 on the Caen Hill flight. This narrowboat is still operational and is popular with sightseers wishing to enjoy a leisurely cruise.

The restoration of the canal includes amenities, canalside resources, and importantly, wildlife habitats along and adjacent to the canal. It is now a popular heritage tourism destination for boating, canoeing, hiking, and an essential cornerstone for wildlife conservation.

In 2011 the Department for Environment, Food and Rural Affairs designated the canal a national cruiseway as per the Transport Act 1968. The designation imposes a legal requirement on British Waterways (today's Canal and River Trust) to maintain the canal to a standard that ensures cruising craft can safely navigate the entire length of the waterway.

The canal acts as a wildlife corridor and offers a variety of habitats for native UK wildlife that otherwise faces the common threat of habitat destruction. One of the big wildlife success stories is the comeback of wild otters in Wiltshire and Berkshire. My first and only sighting to date took place in December 2019 in Wiltshire. We are fortunate to be able to still see these charismatic animals, albeit occasionally, as they very nearly became extinct due to the irresponsible use of pesticides in the 1970s.

Other wildlife that thrives on the canal are kingfishers, water voles, and slow worms. I recently spotted a mink just yards from the boat and while it is classed as a rogue species because it is not native, it was still exciting to see it in the wild.

Some Kennet and Avon Canal trivia.

Since 1991, the Kennet and Avon Canal has been twinned with the French canal, *Les amis du canal du nivernais.*

The second deepest lock in the UK is Bath Deep Lock on this system and it measures 19ft 5ins (6 metres) deep.

The most iconic structure on the canal is the Caen Hill Flight, a series of 16 locks that ascend 130ft 8 ins (40 metres) in just 0.62 miles (1 kilometre). This flight is part of a total of 29 locks through Devizes that elevate the canal 240ft over the course of just 2 miles.

There are a number of aqueducts of which the two best known are Avoncliff and Dundas.

Events hosted on the canal include the Bristol Harbour Festival, International Devizes to Westminster Canoe Race, Newbury Waterways Festival, Newbury Crafty Craft Race, Reading Water Fest, Saltford Regatta.

GLOSSARY

Aft cabin	a boat's rear bedroom
Air draft	the height of the boat from the waterline
Beam	the width of a boat at its widest
Bilge	the compartment below decks where water often pools
Boat safety certificate	Essential requirement on British inland waterways - see appendix for more detail
Bollard	a mushroom-shaped iron post used to tie a boat's mooring lines to
Bow	the front end of the boat
Bulkhead	a dividing wall between a boat's cabins
Cabin cruiser	a motorboat with accommodation facilities
Calorifier	a hot water storage tank
Cleats	t-shaped pins on the boat used to secure ropes and fenders to
Cockpit	location of the main steering and instrument panel.
Draft	the depth of the boat's hull below the waterline
Elsan	a sewerage disposal facility named after the Elsan chemical toilet
Fender	rubber bumpers hung along the sides of boats
Fore cabin	a boat's forward bedroom
Gunwale	the upper edge of a boat's hull
Galley	a boat's kitchen
Head	a boat's shower and toilet
Liveaboards	people who live primarily onboard boats
Lock paddles	the sluice gates used to fill and empty a closed lock
Lock gates	the beam gates used to close a lock
Lock cil	a concrete step under upper gates of locks

Narrowboat	a long narrow boat designed to fit in the locks on British canal systems
Port side	the left side of boat (facing forward)
Saloon	a boat's dining cabin
Skin fitting	the seal around an outlet in a boat's hull
Starboard	right side of boat facing forward
Stern	the rear of a boat
Tender	a rowboat or dinghy used to ferry to and from a larger vessel
Vanlifers	people who live in vans and campervans
WD-40	brand of water displacement lubricant
Weil's disease	a bacterial infection, leptospirosis, often caught through contact with contaminated fresh water
Widebeam	a narrowboat style vessel, but with a width of 7ft 1in (2metres) or more.
Winding hole	a widening on the canal to enable narrowboats to turn about
Winter mooring	moorings made available for a cost per meter from November to the end of February
Yoghurt Pot	UK slang term for a boat made of glass reinforced plastic (GRP)

USEFUL ITEMS

The following is a list of items we find useful, even essential, for living comfortably on Wyebourne. You can find more information on most of these products on our webpage at www.jglennbauer.co.uk/offgrid-boaters as well links to retailers who may supply the items, primarily Amazon. I am a participant in the Amazon Services LLC Associates Program, an affiliate advertising program designed to provide a means to earn fees by linking to Amazon.com and affiliated sites.

Books

- River Thames & the Southern Waterways, Waterways Guide 7

Cabin accessories

- Abode® duvet box-bag sleeping bag

Condensation and waterproofing

- Absorbent condensation drip strips
- 12V Mini dehumidifier
- Grangers Fabsil Gold for oxford cloth canopies
- Crocodile Trading Ltd Dex Camp 3M Tape

Connectivity

- Huawei B535-232 Home/Office Router
- Poynting 4G Antenna

Decorating - exterior

- Toplac brilliant white yacht paint
- Gel coat
- Hammerite 250ml Metal Paint
- International (Yacht) Varnish Original 750ml
- Wood Oil

Decorating - interior

- Arthome 3D Window Privacy Film
- Dryzone anti-mould paint

Electrics

- 12V/24V 3-Socket 120W DC Power Car Splitter
- Portable Inverter Generator
- 5000KW forced air diesel heater
- 400W Power Inverter Car Charger
- Solar-powered security lights
- Vango Photon Headtorch
- Varta Pocket Charger

Galley (Kitchen)

- 12V Hot Cold Portable Electric Cool Box 32L
- Hot water flask
- Jafel iron
- Omni oven
- Pressure cooker

Safety and security

- Car wheel clamp
- Fire extinguishers & fire blanket
- Class B (workplace) first aid kit
- Gas detector alarm (propane/butane/methane gas detector)
- Life Saver Carbon Monoxide Alarms
- Smoke Alarms
- Video alarm
- Wireless Vibration Alarm

Solar power system

- 12V 120AH Deep Cycle Leisure Marine Batteries
- 20A 12V/24V MPPT solar charge controller
- Monocrystalline solar panel
- Leisure Battery Holding Boxes

Toilet and shower system

- Porta Potti 335 Portable Toilet
- Chemical toilet fluid & rinse

APPENDIX

Listed here are some of the basics that we have learned while living as off-grid boaters. This section could be described as a checklist for readers who are considering a life on the water.

Boat insurance: Boats must first be insured in order to be licenced by the Canal and River Trust or Environment agency.

Boat licence: All boats must be licenced to use the waterways by the Canal and River Trust. This includes everything from canoe to houseboat and regardless of whether it has a motor or not. Cost is dependent on the length of the vessel and before a licence will be issued, the boat must have a valid insurance and BSS certificate.

Boat safety scheme: The Boat Safety Scheme (BSS) is an initiative by both the Environment Agency and the Canal and River Trust. Its purpose is to minimise risks to life and property, including the environment. BSS certification is like a motor vehicle MOT (UK) and all boats must undergo inspection by a certified independent assessor every four years. The inspection will include all fuel and power systems onboard to reduce the risk of fires, explosions, and pollution.

Boat sales: These are the websites we trawled when we were shopping for our boat. This is not a recommendation for their services, and we do not accept any responsibility for the outcome of your interaction with any of the listed sites.

- Apolloduck.co.uk
- Boatshed.com
- Boatshop24.co.uk

Breakdown and rescue insurance: Great for peace of mind, this is an optional one-off annual insurance that covers your boat in the case of breakdown or even sinking.

Continuous cruising: Where boats do not have a residential mooring, they are required to continuously cruise. To fulfil the terms of continuous cruising, boaters are expected to cruise a minimum distance of twenty miles in a year. Boaters may not remain in one place for more than fourteen days and should not return to an area where they have recently moored. The following website is the route planner we used to plan our journey down the Thames.

- Canalplan.co.uk

Diesel heater: Diesel heaters are effective heating generating systems. They are popular in trucks where they are wired into the electrics and feed from the fuel tank. Low cost diesel heaters from China have seen diesel heater popularity increase among boaters whereas before, expensive German makes made this option less viable. The downside is they draw a lot of power from the battery bank.

HETAS: Is the organisation in the UK which drives safety in the use of biomass and other solid fuels. HETAS standards should be used in the installation of wood burners on boats as these are applied when undergoing the BSS certification.

Leisure battery basics: Leisure batteries are intended to deliver low currents over sustained periods before being recharged slowly. Every time a battery is discharged it sustains wear which compromises its capacity to hold a charge. Leisure batteries are built to better withstand frequent deep discharge of power. Ideally a leisure battery should be discharged no lower than a battery voltage reading of 12.4V, which is about half its capacity.
Common leisure batteries are lead-acid types and their

capacity is measured in ampere hours (AH). I have three 95ah leisure batteries installed in a battery bank on Wyebourne.

Solar power basics: Solar panels and charger controllers are not difficult to install if you have some DIY experience or are a quick learner. The benefit of solar power is you have a cheap semi-reliable source of free energy straight into your boat. Unlike generators, a solar array will recharge your battery bank silently and with no pollution. You can buy solar kits that have all the necessary components, or you can mix and match, but here is the primary gear you will need:

Solar panels: These range from 50W to 150W. For heavy use, you will need panels amounting to 300W. Monocrystalline solar panels currently convert light to energy more efficiently than the poly or thin-film panels. Thin film panels are flexible panels that can be fixed to roofs of boats and campervans with adhesives.

Solar wiring: Positive and negative solar cable that connects to the solar panel to the charge controller. Separate to the cables, you will also need a fused harness that connects the charge controller to the battery bank.

Solar charge controller: There are two types; PWM (pulse width modulation) and MPPT (Maximum Power Point Tracking). The MPPT is recommended by specialists, especially for bigger kits, and is more expensive.

OTHER TITLES

By J. Glenn Bauer

Sons of Iberis Series

Warhorn, Book 1
Battle Cloud, Book 2
Gladius Winter, Book 3
Howl of Blades, Book 4
Broken Shield, Book 5 (date to be advised)

Prequel to Sons of Iberia

Rise of the Spears

Others

The Runeovex Secret
Von Steiner's Gold

CHILDREN'S BOOKS BY VALLEY KINGHORN

Peanut and Popcorn. The Bandit Seagull
Crazy Candy
Mr Spud, Wild Wild West

www.jglennbauer.co.uk

Printed in Great Britain
by Amazon